THE
HiSTORY
MAKERS

Pitch Publishing Ltd
A2 Yeoman Gate
Yeoman Way
Durrington
BN13 3QZ

Email: info@pitchpublishing.co.uk
Web: www.pitchpublishing.co.uk

First published by Pitch Publishing 2017
Text © 2017 Sarah Juggins and Richard Stainthorpe

1

A CIP catalogue record for this book is available from the British Library.

13-digit ISBN: 9781785313301
Design and typesetting by Olner Pro Sport Media.
Print Managed by Jellyfish Print Solutions.

TEAM GB

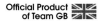

Official Product
of Team GB

THE HISTORY MAKERS

How Team GB Stormed to a
First Ever Gold in Women's Hockey

Sarah Juggins and Richard Stainthorpe

Foreword by Dame Katherine Grainger DBE

Chair of UK Sport, 2012 Olympic gold medallist and winner of a further four silver Olympic medals in a career spanning five Olympic Games.

Each Olympic Games creates moments of pure magic. There are scenes that are played over and over again as the years roll by, standing the test of time. Something about them captures the essence of sport: the gladiatorial competition, the collaboration, the glorious victory or crushing defeat, the burning desire, the spirit of humanity. Many times these magic moments are defined not only by the day in question, but also by the journey taken to arrive at that place.

Team GB women's hockey team's golden win in Rio 2016 is one of those moments and will rightly be remembered and celebrated. In the fading light of a warm Brazilian evening they battled through 60 minutes of match play and then raised their game in a penalty shootout, while a nation held its breath. But beyond that moment is a tale that involves a wider cast of characters and a broader range of emotions. Rio 2016 was only the last step of a long journey that Team GB women's hockey had been on. Further back along that road is the shadow of heartbreak and disappointment, of self-doubt and frustration. Such feelings and emotions cut deep and often last far longer than the thrill of victory. For some, those emotions sadly might last forever; for some lucky others they can be used to motivate and push forward.

The past five Olympic Games that some of the Team GB women's hockey team were part of also tracked my own Olympic time and I vividly remember sitting in a hotel reception in Italy where the Team GB rowing team were on training camp in 2004. The Olympic hockey qualification for Athens 2004 was being streamed online and a group of us were huddled around a laptop, entranced. When Team GB suffered their shock defeat at the hands of Korea there was a cumulative intake of breath. Someone asked what next for the team; how could they qualify now? The haunting silence that followed answered the question. There were no more chances. Their Olympic dream was over before it had begun.

Fast forward eight years and I was at the Riverbank Arena in the London Olympic Park for Team GB's final two matches of the 2012 Olympic Games. What a contrast of emotions was demonstrated in those two games. The heartbreak was palpable when Team GB lost their semi-final against Argentina. My memories are still strong of every Team GB hockey player collapsing to their knees knowing the dream of the gold medal was now out of reach. But sport tests character and the strong can survive and flourish. The spirit and fierce determination of the 2012 team saw them return for the bronze medal match and the joy of winning a medal in that Olympic cauldron perhaps hinted at what more would come. The fire was stoked, the game was on, and Rio 2016 would take things to a new level.

Watching from the stands in Rio, I was with a large British contingent who were hoarse by the end of the night from the vocal support given. We knew this was the just reward for a job very well done. And beyond the personal pride was the overwhelming knowledge that their result would now reach far and wide, inspiring old and young to perhaps do something, try something, take on a challenge, overcome a disappointment, plant a seed of what might be or simply make people proud.

This is the story of ordinary people, who harnessed their incredible skills and set about to achieve something extraordinary together. Some were fuelled by the past, some excited by the future, all driven to create their own piece of history and inspire as many as possible along the way. Coaches, support staff, management, past players, friends, family and fans all played vital roles and can rightfully share in the celebration.

This is the story of how Team GB women's hockey team cemented their place in Olympic history, united a nation, inspired a multitude and created their own moment of pure magic.

◄ **Georgie Twigg celebrates at London 2012.**
Frank Uijlenbroek

Photographer biographies

The majority of the images that appear within the pages of this book were taken by Dutchmen Frank Uijlenbroek and Koen Suyk, two of the world's leading hockey photographers.

Frank Uijlenbroek
Frank has travelled the globe taking images of the sport, supplying various agencies, newspapers and major online news outlets as well as National Associations, Continental Federations and the International Hockey Federation (FIH). Frank has 25 years' experience in the business, and was on hand to capture the hockey images at the Beijing 2008, London 2012 and Rio 2016 Olympic Games. Frank is the owner of the FFU Press Agency and World Sport Pics.

Koen Suyk
A veteran of eight Olympic Games, Koen has captured some of the sport's most iconic moments. Over a 40-year career he has earned a reputation as a world class photographer working for agencies such as Reuters, ANP and ANEFO (Amsterdam). At the Rabobank Hockey World Cup in 2014, the Royal Dutch Hockey Association (KNHB) honoured Koen by creating a public display of some of his finest images, while a famous shot of Alex Danson in full flight was named Best Photo at the 2015 EuroHockey Championships in London.
    The authors wish to express our sincere gratitude for supporting this project.

◀ Passion, desire, determination
and unity were on show for all
to see at Rio 2016.
Frank Uijlenbroek.

How Great Britain Hockey works and the importance of GB Primacy

On 9 May 2006, the Great Britain Hockey Business and Performance Framework Agreement was signed between the national governing bodies of the three home nations: England, Scotland and Wales. This groundbreaking accord was developed following a steady decline in British performances in Olympic competition, the highest level of hockey, after 1996.

This legally binding document is built around the central concept of Great Britain Primacy, meaning that all three nations are fully committed to putting the ultimate performance goal of Team GB's men's and women's hockey teams achieving Olympic success ahead of everything else.

As part of the agreement, a nominated national governing body from the three nations leads the delivery of the Great Britain hockey teams' business operations and performance objectives, preparing the teams for the Olympic Games. The nominated country is appointed every Olympic cycle against agreed criteria. This responsibility is held by England Hockey, who have been the nominated national governing body for each Olympic cycle since the signing of the framework agreement. As such, England Hockey lead the business and performance operations relating to GB Hockey.

The Great Britain Hockey Business and Performance Framework Agreement has been one of the most significant factors in the rise of Team GB over the last ten years, allowing a new level of commitment and understanding to develop between the home nations, putting the athletes at the very centre of a programme designed to maximise the chances of success for Team GB at Olympic level.

While the home nations regularly compete in international competitions as separate entities, in the two-year cycle that leads up to an Olympic Games it is Team GB that competes in top level events such as the Olympic qualifiers, Champions Trophy and, of course, the Olympic Games itself.

Complete information about the GB Framework agreement can be found on www.greatbritainhockey.co.uk

Author acknowledgements

The authors would like to offer our sincere gratitude to the athletes (both past and present) and coaching staff for their assistance with this book. Thanks to Sally Munday and her staff at England / Great Britain Hockey with a special mention to the excellent Beth Moorley, as well as former chief executive Philip Kimberley. We would also like to acknowledge the following people for their invaluable guidance: Sophie Stainthorpe, Malcolm Croft, Nick Irvine, Colin Pike, Peter Luck, the late Peter Savage as well as Jane Camillin and everyone at Pitch Publishing for backing this project. A huge thank you to Dame Katherine Grainger for enthusiastically agreeing to write the foreword for this book. Finally, we cannot forget to show our appreciation to our partners, Dawn Course and Donna Reynolds, as well as our parents, Roger and Brenda Juggins and Michael and Christine Stainthorpe, for their unwavering patience and support.

Dedication
A project like this is only possible with the support of the, by now renowned, Hockey Family. We would like to dedicate this book to some special members of the Hockey Family who would have liked to see the story through to its end, but who were tragically taken from us too early – Graham and Tom Wilson, Peter Savage and Peter Hogg.

Great Britain struggled at the elite Hockey Champions ▶
Trophy 2016 competition in London, where the team
finished fifth, just six weeks prior to Rio 2016.
Frank Uijlenbroek.

Prologue

Friday 19 August 2016

As the cameras panned onto the 16 women standing on the podium, gold medals around their necks, the emotions were as individual as the personalities. For some, there were expressions of disbelief; for others it was sheer joy; the huge smiles on the faces of Laura Unsworth, Georgie Twigg and Hollie Webb; the defiant celebration of Lily Owsley; the unmasked shock of Sam Quek; the quiet satisfaction of a job well done from Sophie Bray. And for married couple Kate and Helen Richardson-Walsh, it was the pinnacle of two international careers that had spanned the best part of two decades. These were the moments when a tight-knit group of players, who had trained, played and lived together in the most intensive of times, finally allowed the masks to slip. This was what they had prepared for, this was what the tough training, the tears, the aching muscles, the uncompromising search for excellence had boiled down to. This was it, this was their moment.

Tuesday 23 August 2016

British Airways 747, flight number BA2016, repainted with a golden nose and renamed 'victoRIOus' carries the squad home from Rio to London. Moments after landing, footage filmed by track sprinter and 4x100m bronze medallist Asha Philip goes viral on social media, showing the hockey girls belting out the British National Anthem with pride and passion, before bursting into a plane-shaking rendition of Gala's 1997 dance hit 'Freed From Desire'.

Upon entering the arrivals hall, the players are amazed to find not just family and friends waiting to greet them, but dozens of members of the public. The next few days are a frenzy of press receptions, television appearances, radio interviews and photoshoots.

'It was absolutely bonkers,' recalls Hannah Macleod. 'Wherever you turned there were people wanting to speak to you, to hug you. It was overwhelming. You certainly don't go round saying you're an Olympic champion and it still sounds strange

Golden moment as Team GB's women's hockey squad and coaching staff celebrate Olympic glory at Rio 2016.
Frank Uijlenbroek.

Team GB pose for photographers after their shootout victory over the Netherlands in the women's Hockey final at the Rio 2016 Olympic Games.
Frank Uijlenbroek

saying it, but we haven't stopped since; our feet haven't touched the ground.

'We probably won't know the true extent (of what we have achieved) for another couple of years and if we get another medal-winning team in 12 years' time it would be amazing to hear they were inspired by 2016. I think we have now truly evolved from the "Jolly hockey sticks era".'

September 2016

Maddie Hinch may have been one of the heroes on the pitch but, since landing back in the UK the goalkeeper has become a media sensation, from a show-stealing appearance alongside Rene Zellweger on *The Jonathan Ross Show* to taking her place on the couch on the BBC's flagship programme, *The One Show*. She says: 'Since landing back in Britain, everything has started to hit home. We were in a bubble for three weeks; we had no idea what was going on at home. After winning gold, the first thing my brother texted me was, "Maddie, you're trending on Twitter", not "Well done on the gold".

'BBC television's viewing figures for the Olympic final were something like nine million, which is incredible. I am glad I didn't know that before the game. It would have made it even more daunting.

'Coming back home and seeing the number of people in the airport, little kids with hockey sticks and team kits ... that was the moment when it hit home. They seemed to be in awe of us and wanted to be us.'

———————

While the Team GB squad and coaching staff basked in the glory of a gold medal and the adulation of a British public that has taken them into their hearts, there is not a person involved with the squad who has not also experienced the other side of top class competition. If ever a team has been at either end of a spectrum, it is this squad. For most of the players, the pain has been recent. Just six weeks prior to Rio, Great Britain finished fifth out of six in front of a home crowd at the 2016 Champions Trophy in London, leaving many to seriously question what possible chance they had of medalling in Brazil. Many of the squad represented England at the World Cup 2014 in the Netherlands, travelling to The Hague ranked third in the world only to endure a woeful tournament and suffer an 11th place finish. That pain is hard to erase, but for three members of the squad the tough times started much earlier, enduring the most torrid of times at the start of their international careers.

For Helen Richardson-Walsh a bright start as the youngest player to represent Team GB women's hockey at an Olympics, being just 18 at Sydney 2000, was soon overshadowed by a series of career-threatening injuries which kept her out of the game for months on end. Meanwhile, for captain Kate Richardson-Walsh and fellow defender Crista Cullen, the lowest point of their careers had taken place during an Olympic qualifier in New Zealand in 2004 – an event that Helen missed as she was fighting back from injury.

March 2004

'Devastated, humiliated, felt like walking away from the sport.' These were the sentiments of Kate Richardson-Walsh – then simply Kate Walsh prior to her marriage to Helen Richardson in 2013 – just 24 hours after the Team GB women's hockey team had crashed spectacularly out of the Olympic qualifiers in Auckland, losing 2-0 to Korea in a must-win battle in the chase for fifth place and a spot at Athens 2004.

Helen Richardson was also an Olympic debutant at Sydney 2000.
Stu Forster / Getty Images

Kate Walsh in action for Team GB at the Sydney 2000 Olympic Games.
Shaun Botterill / Getty Images

This was the first time Team GB women had failed to qualify for the Olympics since they had first entered the competition in 1988 and it was a miserable start to Kate's tenure as captain of her national side. The young defender had been named captain just a few months earlier and, with revered Australian coach Tricia Heberle at the helm, this was supposed to signal a brave new world for Great Britain women's hockey. The coach had introduced a new attacking style, backed up with improved fitness and skill levels as well as a psychologist to calm jittery nerves. This was paying dividends as the team climbed up the world rankings to fifth in the world. The Olympic qualifier should have been a formality. The top five teams would have an automatic passage to Athens and Great Britain were the highest-ranked team in Auckland for the event.

Over the course of the ten-day tournament, the hopes and dreams of the players were cruelly dashed. Team GB failed miserably to play to their potential. True, they beat two teams in the pool matches – Ukraine and Ireland – but a draw with New Zealand and a loss to Germany meant they finished third in the pool matches. This left them out of the race to the podium and contesting fifth to eighth place in the crossover matches. Their first opponents were Korea and everyone knew that only a victory against the Asian side would give Team GB the chance to play for that all-important fifth place. In the event, early goals from Kim Jin-Kyoung and Park Jeong-Sook saw the Team GB challenge fade to nothing. They finished seventh after a dismally unsatisfying 2-0 win over Ireland, returning home to a barrage of criticism from the media and the wider public.

Kate Walsh, Crista Cullen and Sarah Thomas crestfallen at the Beijing 2008 Olympic Games.
Aamir Qureshi / Getty Images

'Those feelings (of devastation) will never go away,' says Crista Cullen. 'Missing out on an Olympic Games that you have trained so hard for is an incredibly hard position to find yourself in. As a youngster, I was lucky, I got to go to the Junior World Cup and get away from it all. Many of the players retired on the back of that performance, that was a very hard time.'

For Kate it was a seminal moment: 'Looking back on that time, I think that may be where I first began to build my inner strength,' she says. 'Over time I have become a firm believer that, in order to succeed, you really have to plumb the depths and understand what it is to lose. That is the only way you can really appreciate what it takes to win.'

And, as Kate and Crista have discovered, it is not just about learning to lose but having the patience to wait for their time to come. It has taken a full 12 years for the two Olympians to wipe away the stains of that time in Auckland.

2004-2008

The seeds of change began in the build up to Beijing 2008. In 2003, Danny Kerry started working with the England 'A' squad. The coach, who had previously coached Premier League side Canterbury, was swiftly promoted to take charge of England Senior Women on 1 January 2005 and then, in 2007, he was appointed as head coach to Great Britain Women's squad, giving him just a few months to prepare for Beijing 2008. The event was not an unqualified success, with Team GB finishing sixth and many questions being asked about the suitability of a new young coach, with limited international experience. As Kerry himself says: 'I was horribly naive and horribly inexperienced,' but he was also quick to learn and had an insatiable desire to improve every aspect of his coaching.

And, Beijing apart, Kerry's tenure was yielding a steady stream of results. During the period 2005-2010, his teams – England and Great Britain – amassed ten medals at European, Commonwealth and World level. This included a first ever podium finish, a bronze medal, at the 2010 World Cup.

Beijing 2008 may not have been a glorious triumph but it was an improvement on what had gone before. Team GB finished sixth, which was well above their world ranking coming into the tournament. But, as Kerry admitted, he had a lot to learn and Beijing was just the first step along a much longer journey. It would take time for the new coach to develop and then share his vision, although the steady haul of medals and the slow but steady climb back up the rankings was all that the bosses at England Hockey and UK Sport needed as proof to the wisdom of their selection.

August 2012

By the time London 2012 came around, Kerry's ideas were beginning to bear fruit and the exploits of the hockey women began to capture the public's imagination. A bronze medal in London was almost overshadowed by the horrific injury suffered by Kate Walsh. For an all too short time, the women's hockey team was all over the media as captain Kate, with her jaw wired up, led her team to the second bronze medal in their history, adding to the one claimed by Jane Sixsmith and co. at Barcelona 1992 some 20 years previous.

Across the UK, people were suddenly seeing hockey in the newspapers, front page and back; players were being interviewed on radio and television; and suddenly hockey players such as Alex Danson and Kate Walsh were becoming household names. The presence of Catherine, Duchess of Cambridge at several matches, plus a photoshoot in *Hello* magazine, showing the Duchess holding a hockey stick and chatting to the players, did wonders for the team's profile.

As Team GB took the game to New Zealand in that bronze medal match, there were signs the team that Kerry had envisaged was emerging. Despite a devastating loss to Argentina in the semi-final, tough mental resilience and belief in each other was beginning to blossom. London had in many ways arrived too early.

Speaking to *The Guardian* newspaper, joint-leading goalscorer at the tournament Crista Cullen said: 'A gold medal was what we had spoken about for so many years and that was what it was about, but we picked each other up, put our arms round each other ... We said we'd give every ounce of blood out there and that's what we showed today.'

And so began the four year countdown to Rio 2016, which was a rollercoaster journey to say the least. The team experienced victories, losses, fallouts and recriminations but always present, although sometimes hidden very deep, was a belief that this Great Britain squad had the potential to make history.

For Kerry it was all about developing the culture that he had started to put in place after Beijing. 'There were some things that I couldn't change without making too much noise,' explains the coach. 'But there were other things that we could do that would put us in the best possible place to win gold.'

Kerry speaks about marginal gains and attention to every detail. Craig Keegan, the goal-scoring coach, talks about momentum and its importance; Karen Brown, whose main role was coaching the defence, considers the way the team played without the ball as crucial to success; some of the senior players say

Champagne all round on the return flight from Rio 2016, with superstar triathlon gold medallist Alistair Brownlee (bottom right) and gold medal-winning swimmer Adam Peaty (top right) joining the hockey party.
Alex Livesey / Stringer / Getty Images

that learning from losing was the most important thing. Whatever the formula, Team GB got it right in Rio.

And how. Seven games stood between Team GB and a place in the final. Seven games and seven wins. And then the final itself, won in the most dramatic of fashion, after drawing with the world number one team and reigning Olympic champions, the Netherlands in full time. In accordance with hockey regulations, the match went to a shootout – a dramatic one-on-one battle where the attacking player has just eight seconds to score past the goalkeeper. It is gladiatorial in the extreme and is the one time when hockey – fundamentally all about the team – becomes an individual sport where someone can be a hero.

The statistics will show that Team GB won the shootout 2-0, but these stark figures fail to reveal the drama and emotion of that evening.

'It was one of the most unbelievable moments in my life,' says Kate Richardson-Walsh. 'I didn't really know what to feel. On the one hand we had just won a gold medal at the Olympics, the thing that I had aimed for all

my hockey career; but no-one else, no-one outside that tight band of players can even begin to imagine what we had been through to get to that point. I'm not sure anyone ever will.'

While this book is all about celebrating the gold medal that this team of inspirational women won against all the odds on that magical night in Rio de Janeiro, it is also a story of so much more. From those dark days in 2004 when the future of the sport was in doubt, to the highs of Olympic bronze in London 2012. It is the story of coach Danny Kerry's own battle to win over his players and shape them into the squad he wanted them to be, the tactical nous and philosophy he managed to instil into every athlete. It is about those that didn't make the final cut; it is about the injuries that players had to overcome; it is about the mental anguish of being in such a dark place, that picking up a stick and playing the game is the very last thing a player wants to do.

Above all else, this is a book about hope, belief and celebration. All of these players and the support staff have travelled along a turbulent road. As a collective unit they have had to face failure and pick themselves up. They have dreamed of glory only to swallow the bitter pill of defeat. They have turned up to train day-on-day for a sport they always love but sometimes hate with a passion. They have put lives, careers, families and friends on hold, knowing that to lose their focus is to let go of their dream.

This is a story of individuals developing the mental strength to follow through on a vision; having the capacity and humility to be tough and honest when it comes to self-analysis. It is about the realisation that it is not just about self; it is about being able to look team-mates in the eye and know that what is reflected back is a mutual trust.

This book is also unashamedly a celebration. It doesn't deal in cynicism and doubt. You will find no mention in its pages of the legitimacy of pouring lottery money into elite sport; you will not find a discourse about hockey's place in the social fabric of the UK. What you will discover is how an extraordinary group of sportswomen, led by a visionary team of coaches, overturned the odds to put an enormous, collective smile on the face of millions of people in the UK and around the world.

Over the course of the next 14 chapters, we will chart the course of Team GB's journey from the low point of Athens to that golden evening in Rio.

Chapter 1

The Greek Tragedy

As Team GB's women's hockey team prepare for the Tokyo 2020 Olympic Games and seek to achieve head coach Danny Kerry's aspiration to 'win as winners', it seems hard to believe that just over a decade ago, hockey in the UK was at an all-time low. As today's cohort of players embark on a full-time training programme at the National Sports Centre at Bisham Abbey, feted as inspirational heroes across the land and invited to numerous appearances as 'celebrity' sports stars, it is worth looking back to 2004, where the stench of failure was tainting anyone involved in the sport.

For three of the 2016 squad - Crista Cullen, Helen Richardson and Kate Walsh - it was a time when their senior international hockey careers were just getting started. A fourth player, Alex Danson, was also on the cusp of breaking through from the junior squad. While these were unquestionably difficult times for these young members of the Team GB squad, all believe that those experiences contributed to the gold medals that now hang round their necks.

'It was tough being a hockey player in 2004,' says three-times Olympian Crista Cullen, reflecting back to a period in the history of GB women's hockey that now seems like a dreadful nightmare.

In fact, the period around the start of the new century was far from comfortable for anyone involved in the sport, especially in the UK. The national governing body was on the verge of bankruptcy and the national stadium at Milton Keynes was a white elephant around their neck. In terms of international success, a major medal had not been claimed since Team GB's women won bronze at the Barcelona 1992 Olympic Games. England's women enjoyed relative success with silver medals at the 1998 and 2002 Commonwealth Games as well as a gold at the International Hockey Federation's second tier Champions Challenge event, also played in 2002, but the blue riband events were looking like a distant and unrealistic dream.

Sally Munday, the current chief executive officer for England Hockey and chief operating officer of Great Britain Hockey, was a regional development officer at the start of the new millennium. The memory of her beloved sport's decline still causes the normally cheerful CEO to wince. 'In 2002 we discovered the English Hockey Association was going bankrupt. It was hideous, I can't even begin to tell you how it feels when the sport that you love and care about so deeply is going bust. I just remember feeling really, really angry at the people who had led us down this route.'

Two years later, Team GB failed to secure qualification for Athens 2004. It was a devastating situation that deeply affected Munday, with one particular image being permanently burned into their memory. 'We were watching the match updates coming in from Auckland, where the qualifier was taking place,' says Munday. 'The updates were coming through every three minutes or so and it was becoming clear that we were not going to qualify. Then a picture was posted online of Kate (Richardson-Walsh), on her knees, just devastated. I will never forget that image as long as I live.

'I remember thinking, this is the culmination of the sport having been managed badly. I felt this overwhelming sense of purpose that we would never let the athletes end up like this because of poor management.'

Kate Richardson-Walsh recalled that moment in an emotional interview with the BBC's Ollie Williams: 'I still get upset about it now, just having that emotion of... failing. Of not qualifying for an Olympics. That had never happened before.

'I was lucky enough to be a young player, to know – if I was lucky – I'd have another opportunity. But for many players, that was their last chance to represent their

Team GB defender Mel Clewlow shields the ball against host nation New Zealand at the 2004 Women's Hockey Olympic Qualification tournament in Auckland.
Michael Bradley / Getty Images

New Zealand's Suzie Muirhead and Jennie Bimson of Team GB in action at the 2004 Olympic Qualifier.
Michael Bradley / Getty Images

country. When we go out and play now, we play with that in mind. We want to right those wrongs for them.'

The Athens Olympic cycle was a nadir for women's hockey, with the team's dismal failure to qualify for the Olympic Games leaving the morale and self-belief of the players, coaching staff and the governing body at rock bottom. For many players, this was a desperately sad way to end their playing careers and, for head coach Tricia Heberle, it was a blot on a coaching CV that was otherwise first rate.

Australian Heberle had been brought into the coaching set-up to take charge of Great Britain women, following the team's disappointing eighth place finish at Sydney 2000. She was an Olympian herself, representing Australia at the Los Angeles 1984 Olympic Games and had been part of the coaching team that had led the Hockeyroos – the nickname of the Australia women's team – to back-to-back gold medals both at the 1994 and 1998 World Cups and the 1996 and 2000 Olympic Games. Heberle had been coaching England since 2001, so she was a natural and accepted choice for the role.

For the Great Britain squad, under the leadership of Heberle, this was to be a fresh start. Any politics surrounding the sport were firmly the preserve of the national governing body, the athletes were just focused on the qualification. Heberle had guided England to a silver medal at the Manchester 2002 Commonwealth

Games, and within the Great Britain squad the momentum was really starting to build. Climbing to fifth in the world rankings, Great Britain headed to the Olympic qualification tournament in Auckland in March 2004 as the top seeds and with full expectations of securing their ticket to Athens, requiring a top five finish at the ten team event.

At the time, Danny Kerry was a young coach with the England development team and he believed, like everyone else, that Olympic qualification was almost a formality. 'They had been playing well and were rightly favourites for the tournament. But it all went wrong, Tricia resigned and the programme went into a hiatus until October of that year.'

A horrendous qualifying campaign began with a reasonable start, drawing 2-2 in their opening Pool A match against host nation New Zealand. That result was followed by a 2-1 loss to Germany, a team that would eventually go on to take the Olympic title in Athens. Speaking after the Germany defeat, a frustrated Heberle said: 'I am not happy with one point from two games, but we have a quality team and we are playing good hockey. We'll most likely be playing off for fifth to eighth now but we just need to put ourselves in the best form by the end of the week.'

The next two matches saw Team GB record a 1-0 win over lowly-ranked Ukraine, followed by a 2-0 victory against near neighbours Ireland. Heberle's prediction proved correct and Team GB found themselves in the fifth to eighth place play-offs, needing to win both matches to qualify.

A strong and very determined Korea took the game to Team GB and, to the amazement of everyone, Korea emerged as 2-0 winners, destroying the Olympic dreams of the Team GB players. Korea would go on to take fifth place, joining Spain, Japan, New Zealand and Germany as the teams to progress through to Athens.

One of the members of the Team GB squad in 2004 was Mel Clewlow, who still plays National League hockey but also commentates on international matches on behalf of the BBC and the International Hockey Federation (FIH). Several years on, there is still a sense of deep regret and bitterness in the defender's voice as she recalls that time.

'I will always remember that qualifying tournament. We were ranked number one going into it and completely believed we would qualify for Athens. Of course, things happen in the build up that you can look back on and think had an impact but we, as the players and the coaching staff, have to take responsibility for what happened.'

For Clewlow, however, a lot of the fault lay at the door of the governing body. 'My own opinion of that time is that, as an England team, we had Trish Heberle as head coach with Ian Jennings as her assistant. This worked well. Trish oversaw the programme and managed the players while Ian delivered the coaching sessions on the pitch. The two of them played to their strengths and, if Ian was pushing us a bit too hard – as he sometimes did – Trish would step in.

'I believe this should have been the Team GB set up as well, but about five months before Auckland, Ian had his contracted hours reduced and subsequently decided not to continue.'

For Clewlow, this is when fractures within the squad began to appear. 'When things started to go wrong the cracks got bigger and bigger to the point where we hit an all-time low. It was made worse because we were in New Zealand and couldn't have been further from home.'

If Clewlow was struggling, for Crista Cullen, then just 18 years of age, it was simply a bewildering time. 'To go through that emotional rollercoaster at that stage and to not gain qualification for Athens, well that was really tough. Not only had we not qualified, but the national governing body was going through some almighty issues as well. We didn't know what direction we were heading in as a group. We were just in an element of disarray.'

Philip Kimberley.
Koen Suyk

Back in England, the new board – led by chief executive Philip Kimberley, a man with a long and distinguished international general management career with Burmah Castrol PLC, and Sally Munday in position as development director – had some serious thinking to do. Munday takes up the narrative: 'Of course we lost 60-70 per cent of our funding across the board – both grass roots and elite level investment. We had been saved from bankruptcy by a loan from businessman Stewart Newton, but the removal of funding by Sport England meant we really had to go back to our roots and think long and hard about what we were going to do.

'Typically for a man with his business acumen, Philip Kimberley kept very calm. He simply said: "We are just going to have to rebuild", and so the performance side began a rebuilding process on the back of that Athens disaster. David Faulkner (an Olympic gold medallist with Team GB at Seoul 1988) had been appointed performance director and he, Philip and myself spent an enormous amount of time writing a performance plan and looking at the things that really needed addressing in the sport.'

Kimberley himself had been horrified at the state hockey was in when he took up the reins. 'There wasn't much information around about what had happened and how bad things had got. When I arrived in 2003, it was very, very bad. There was a very shell-shocked team of people running things and we had a completely new governance structure and a completely new board. We owed £500,000, we had no strategy and we had no financial control. We couldn't even afford a sandwich for a volunteer. At that stage, the elite side was being run by a completely separate organisation called World Class Hockey. And I can tell you, they were a long way from being "world class".'

In 2005, Kimberley managed to re-integrate World Class Hockey back into the fold, and along with Faulkner, the two men put their considerable strategic ability towards re-shaping the performance element.

Prior to Faulkner's appointment, one key move initiated by Kimberley had been the appointment of two young coaches: Danny Kerry was to become head coach to the England women's team, while Jason Lee was appointed as the England men's head coach. Kimberley, who put together the selection panels for the two positions, was very clear about the qualities he was looking for. 'I was pretty clear that I wanted coaches with brains, who could work up a learning curve. I felt that the coaches had to be English or British because the cultural nuances offered by coaches from abroad were just not working.'

Kerry recounts the events surrounding his appointment. 'The job as senior coach to England came up and Mike Hamilton was outgoing performance director. I asked whether it was worth me applying and he was typically honest. He told me to apply, but really it was just good experience and a chance to get my cv together. He certainly wasn't optimistic of my chances.

'At the same time the chance to apply as head coach to Scotland came up, so I sent my cv off for that one too.

'I spent a lot of time on my cv, I thought very hard about what to write and then I printed it out on really top class paper. I went through the first round for England and then I was invited to the first round for Scotland. Then, as I was invited to the second round for England, I got offered the Scotland job.

'It certainly helped my cause that Scotland had offered me the job. It also helped that we had recently had a string of foreign coaches, so it was a case of "do we pay for an established foreign coach or invest in a young English coach?" I think a set of circumstances helped my cause.'

As Kerry and Lee took up their respective positions, the men were ranked tenth in the FIH World Rankings, while the women had slipped to 11th. 'Our aim,' says Munday, 'was to move up the rankings, one place per year.'

However, the true game-changer for both England Hockey and GB Hockey came on 6 July 2005,

Sally Munday.
Peter Savage

when London was named as the host city of the 2012 Olympic Games. 'That felt like an unbelievable moment,' says Munday. 'We now knew we had seven years to get things right from a performance perspective but we also wanted to use a home Olympic Games to grow the sport and have an impact on the wider sport. That was where our culture of "inspiring a generation" was born.'

And so the new England Hockey Board set about implementing the new strategy, and the first task was to win back the trust of the grass roots hockey players – this was to be the tentative first step towards creating the Hockey Family. To build trust and bridges between the hundreds of clubs in the UK, Munday and Kimberley got out and about, spending days meeting and talking to people involved in all levels of hockey. 'We were faced by tremendous hostility to start with,' recalls Kimberley. 'In Sally and myself, you have two very stubborn people. We were determined to drag people with us.'

While the grass roots were being wooed by Munday and Kimberley, at performance level, politics was still proving an issue. All the other hockey nations were able to start their Olympic programmes the day after the previous Games had finished. For Great Britain, a unique collaboration between nations that more often than not competed very much as separate entities, this was not the case. It was standard for the Great Britain coach to be appointed just nine months before the start of the Olympic Games, although occasionally this was extended to a year in advance, if they were lucky.

Even after the appointment of a head coach, things were far from simple. The coach was expected to take a large group of players to test events to ensure they were seen to be giving everyone a fair chance. The team would finally get down to its preparations with about six months to go, which was far from ideal.

Alex Danson shows her striker's instinct to score against New Zealand's Black Sticks at the Beijing 2008 Olympic Games.
Frank Uijlenbroek.

To counter this disadvantage, Kimberley developed the concept of the Great Britain Framework, a legally binding document that after months of intense negotiations was finally agreed and signed in 2006 by the three home nations: England, Scotland and Wales.

It was built around an underlying structure called Great Britain Primacy, meaning that all three nations committed to putting the ultimate goal of Team GB achieving Olympic success ahead of everything else. A nominated country would have full and complete responsibility to lead the delivery of the Great Britain hockey teams' business operations and performance objectives, preparing the teams for the Olympic Games. The nominated country would be named at the start of each Olympic cycle, with England being nominated for each cycle since the framework was signed more than a decade ago.

'I cannot stress enough the significance of that framework agreement and what it has allowed us to do,' says Munday, looking back at what was a new level of commitment and understanding between the home nations. 'It stopped all of the political shenanigans that were going on between England, Scotland and Wales and it has stood the test of time. Great Britain is first and the athletes are at the centre. That fundamentally is what has really changed.'

By 2009, the strategies for change began paying off as England men became European champions. At this point though, the women were still waiting for a breakthrough. A series of third- or fourth-place finishes were promising, but now the ambition was for a second- or first-place finish.

While the women sought silver or gold medals, Faulkner and Kerry began to plot for a Team GB success at the London 2012 Olympic Games. Behind the scenes, Kimberley and the board were doing their bit by securing the rights to host the 2010 Champions Trophy.

This was important from both a commercial and a performance standpoint. While hosting home games would spark public interest and be interesting to sponsors, for the coach, it was an important opportunity for the players to get used to playing in front of home crowds, otherwise they could be overwhelmed when it came to London 2012.

The first chance to host a home event came in 2010 with the Champions Trophy being held in Nottingham. It couldn't have gone much better. England competed in the event and took the bronze medal, beating Germany by a 2-1 scoreline. Importantly, the home crowd gave England's athletes a small but significant indication of the level of support they could expect should they represent Team GB in two years' time.

The Champions Trophy success was quickly followed by another significant milestone as England claimed a first ever World Cup bronze medal at the 2010 event in Rosario, Argentina.

Munday laughs as she recalls the World Cup medal. 'We were reliant on another result to get through to the semi-finals, so I was getting a coffee with Danny (Kerry) and Karen (Brown) in a cafe in Rosario because we couldn't face watching the game. Craig Parnham (assistant coach) was watching and he sent us text messages throughout the game to update us.

'When he texted the final result, and we realised we were into the semi-finals, we were jumping around the cafe and hugging each other. All the locals thought we had gone mad.'

That moment, says Munday, is when the England squad which would make up the bulk of the team that would compete at London 2012 really began to believe that they had a chance of winning an

Crista Cullen scored three times at Beijing 2008, including the winner against New Zealand in the pool phase.
Frank Uijlenbroek

Olympic medal. 'I honestly don't think that they believed they were good enough until then.'

For Crista Cullen and Kate Richardson-Walsh – then simply known as Kate Walsh prior to her marriage to international team-mate Helen Richardson – the pain suffered in 2004 is something that will haunt them for ever. Helen Richardson-Walsh missed the trip as she was suffering the first of many back injuries, while teenager Alex Danson was very much a junior on the cusp of the squad. All of them have spoken individually about the experience and the inner strength that came from those difficult times, especially when it comes to dealing with subsequent events. And, as one, they attribute their success in Rio with the failures suffered by the Great Britain squad of 2004.

It is a point with which Mel Clewlow agrees: 'I have to admit, when I look at what the team did in Rio, a little part of me thinks, "yes, I played my part in that", I truly believe that those difficult times were the catalyst for a huge change in both England Hockey and its structure and the attitude and culture surrounding the players.'

For Clewlow, it was not the end of her international career, but she struggled to get over the disappointment. She took time away from the international game before returning to the fold and playing at Beijing 2008. 'It was horrific not to qualify and I personally took some time out of the international game as I felt disillusioned after this. It sounds dramatic, but I needed to reassess my life. It was a harsh and very honest debriefing process but looking back now, hitting rock bottom in 2004 helped start the rebuilding process that led to gold in Rio.'

Once they returned from Auckland, Crista Cullen returned to the England U21 squad to play in the Junior World Cup in Santiago, Chile. It was the break from the senior set-up she needed, but now she looks back, she reflects on how the older members of the squad must have felt. 'Being the youngster in the team, there is an element of lack of responsibility. I was the new kid on the block. But there was also that ingrained respect for the other athletes who have achieved a huge amount.

'I was a whippersnapper brought in mainly because of my physical attributes rather than my ability to play hockey, if we are being genuinely honest. I was in a relatively luxurious position, going to Chile was a good time to get the experience of Auckland out of my mind as quickly as possible. Not all the athletes had that same luxury. I think it was a really hard time to get non-

Victory lap following England's bronze medal triumph over Germany at the 2010 Hockey World Cup in Rosario, Argentina.

Sally Walton and Ashleigh Ball celebrate England's bronze medal at the 2010 Women's Hockey World Cup in Rosario, Argentina, where goals from Alex Danson and Helen Richardson sealed victory over Germany.
Frank Uijlenbroek

qualification. A lot of athletes retired on that. It was a very disappointing campaign, and those emotions and feelings will never go away. Missing out on an Olympic Games that you have trained so hard for – no matter what your age – is, I think, an incredibly hard position to be in.

'Dealing with disappointment and coming from rock bottom is fundamental for an athlete gaining success. I think that, unless you know what it is like to

have been in the worst possible position, you don't have the fundamental blocks to build on. As much as it is a terribly hard, emotional nightmare from a sporting context to be going through, I think it did stand us in quite good stead. If you do exactly what you don't want to do, which is not gain qualification, then I think that you do have to take a good hard look at yourself and you learn a lot about yourself and others.'

A semi-final defeat at the hands of the Netherlands ended England's title hopes at the 2010 Women's Hockey World Cup in Rosario, Argentina.
Frank Uijlenbroek

The athletes parade at the Opening Ceremony of the London 2012 Olympic Games. *Frank Uijlenbroek*

When London won the right to host the 2012 Olympic Games, the England Hockey Board, led by chair Philip Kimberley and chief executive Sally Munday, saw a fantastic opportunity to put hockey on the map not just in England but across the UK. The next seven years was a maelstrom of activity as England Hockey set off on a road trip to sell hockey to the masses. Everyone was involved: clubs, schools, players past and present. Hockey went from the traditional 11-a-side game to an amalgamation of versions, all aimed towards one target – raising the sport's profile. Munday's stated aim was to make hockey a sport that 'mattered' to people.

Among the sport's many iterations were: Quicksticks, a small-sided game designed to attract the 7-11 age group; Back to Hockey, which aimed to get adults back into a sport they might not have played for years; Rush Hockey was a 5-a-side version of hockey for adults; the East London project FRE flyers, looked to get the kids living in the London boroughs hosting the Olympics into hockey. Whether it was being sold as a fun activity to get adults fit, a workplace-based sport that helped team building, or a cool, exciting urban activity

for teenagers, hockey was bravely setting out to win hearts and minds across the country.

There was even a giant hockey ball, which went on a Big Dribble, covering 2,012km from Edinburgh to Trafalgar Square, visiting schools, clubs and colleges along the way.

That was the fun side of the Olympic countdown. For Sally Munday and her team, this was the golden opportunity to redress the years of uncertainty surrounding the sport's future. But at the heart of England Hockey's hopes for a bright future lay what Munday termed 'the virtuous circle', where international success drives the visibility of the sport, which in turn fuels a growth in participation. As more people take up the sport, so more talent is discovered. For hockey to really secure its future, it had to appeal to the masses but also deliver on the pitch.

England Hockey's virtuous circle was in place, barring one essential component – did we have a chance of international success?

England's medals in 2010 at the Champions Trophy in Nottingham and the World Cup in Rosario, Argentina, had buoyed both the athletes and the coaching staff that would be part of Team GB's shot

The Riverbank Arena enjoyed capacity crowds throughout the London 2012 Olympic Games, and became a cauldron of noise when Team GB were in action.
Frank Uijlenbroek

at Olympic glory. The players were exhilarated at the idea of a home Olympics and, in an early indication of attention to detail, Danny Kerry and his coaches had specifically demanded that the GB team experienced plenty of home fixtures in the build up to London, including regular training on the new Olympic pitch almost from the first moment the turf was laid. 'The Olympic pitch became our home,' says attacker Sarah Thomas. 'We were training while the stands were going up around us, we really felt like it was our pitch.'

Of course, going into a major tournament there are always injury worries and the absence of Alex Danson, Crista Cullen and Thomas at the London Cup just two months prior to the start of the Games caused a few ripples, but Kerry and his team remained upbeat and positive – at least to the outside world.

'There was a brief moment where I wondered if my Olympic dream was over, and it was a nervous wait for the MRI scan on my ankle to come back,' says Crista Cullen as she recalled that time. 'But when it did, the news was good and my rehab began immediately.'

The good news for Team GB was that all three athletes recovered and were available for selection a few weeks later. The bad news was that head coach Danny Kerry now had to cull his squad of players from 28 to 18.

It was an emotional coach who faced the press and the normally reserved Kerry found that he couldn't hold back the tears as he announced his squad of players. 'Words cannot describe how difficult it has been to make the final decision in selecting this squad,' he said. 'Since we centralised our training programme in late 2009, our process has been continuous, making it our most thorough and exhaustive ever. We have chosen what we feel is the best combination of players for the challenges of the Olympic Games. Each and every one of the 28 athletes in the training group has committed so much and as a result we have the most powerful squad spirit I have ever known.'

Alex Danson, talking to the BBC following the squad announcement, was equally overwhelmed, 'It's a huge, unbelievable honour. As a child, and as an athlete you dream of going to an Olympic Games but to have the opportunity in your own country is simply incredible.'

Looking back on that time now, the striker says of selection, 'It is horrible, just horrible. It is supposed to be a happy time but all you can think about is the players who didn't make the squad. It is my least favourite part of the whole process.'

One player whose name would have been first on the team-sheet was goalkeeper Beth Storry. The bubbly shot-stopper emerged as one of the stars of London 2012, so much so that when she retired there was some real panic about who would fill her boots.

She reflects back on the preparations for a home Games: 'One of the things that I loved most about our programme was the planning. After Beijing we sat down as a squad to reflect upon the Olympics and where we wanted to go and what we wanted to achieve.

'Looking back at Beijing, we were all disappointed with coming sixth, yet it was also better than our world ranking going into the tournament. At that point, we decided as a team that we could either stay doing what we were doing and be happy with possibly making or not making the semi-finals, or we can make a change and centralise the programme and push to be the best team in the world and a medal contender at every tournament.

'It was the best decision that we made and, with the support of England Hockey, Sport England and National Lottery funding, we were able to make these changes. It made such a change to us as a squad, to our performances and to our results.

'The first tournament we (England) had was the Champions Trophy in 2009, where we came last, but we all understood that was just us adjusting to the new team and the new members. I think that after that we (England & GB) medalled at every tournament and I would say that it was down to the great improvements we were making as a team after centralising our programme. It brought us together as a team, sure we grew in terms of our fitness, but most importantly, we grew as a team and as a squad. I think that was the thing that really helped our medals in London and Rio – we were such a tight squad – it was always about the bigger picture, all the athletes, not just those on the bus to the Olympics.'

And so the London 2012 Olympic Games got underway and it provided all the drama, incident and excitement that it had promised, especially for the 16,000 fans who packed the stands surrounding the distinctive blue and pink 'Smurf turf' at the Riverbank Arena every day. Action got underway every morning and the hockey was still going on – fast, furious and thrilling – late into the night, even as fans drifted away from the other iconic stadiums.

Over 14 days, 24 teams – 12 men's and 12 women's – battled towards the podium. For Team GB's men and women, playing in front of the exuberant crowds was both exciting and daunting.

'We tried to prepare ourselves in the best way possible, but walking out for that first match was insane,' says Thomas, who was the sole Welsh player on the Team GB squad. 'I had been to one Olympics (Beijing) and loved it, but this was a totally different experience.'

Thomas retired from international hockey after London 2012, largely because the 2014 World Cup cycle meant that, with Wales unlikely to qualify, she wouldn't

Captain courageous. Kate Walsh in action against China, just days after breaking her jaw.
Frank Uijlenbroek

have any major tournaments for two years. Although admitting that she sometimes misses being part of the international squad, to this day her memory of that first walk out in London still gives her goosebumps.

For Team GB, it couldn't have started any better, or any worse. A 4-0 win over Japan, with Alex Danson scoring the first and fourth goal and Sarah Thomas and Sally Walton adding to the tally gave Team GB the start they wanted but, during the game, a horrific injury to captain Kate Walsh saw the defender leaving the ground in an ambulance, clutching her jaw.

The next morning's papers were full of images of the stricken player and the team learnt that she had a badly fractured jaw that would need a plate to hold it in place. The question on the minds of both the coaching team and the wider hockey audience was how the rest of the squad would cope with the loss of their inspirational captain?

'To lose your captain in the first game could have really broken the team,' says Storry as she reflects back. 'We could have lost focus and I think that was testament to how we were as a group, that yes, you felt it, but we stuck to the task and stayed focussed and got on with it.'

Thomas agrees. 'We were all thinking about Kate and the fact we had lost our captain, and of course we were worried for Helen (Richardson, Kate's partner) and how she would be feeling. But we had to come together as professionals and get on with the job in hand.'

Nevertheless, it was a slightly subdued Team GB who took to the field a day later to battle it out with an

Georgie Twigg scores against Korea before wheeling away in celebration.
Frank Uijlenbroek

obdurate Korea. Nicola White gave Team GB an early 1-0 lead but Korea came back quickly. The game went back and forth and, with just over ten minutes to play, the score stood at 3-3, with Danson and Cullen the other GB scorers. Goals from Georgie Twigg and Chloe Rogers took it to 5-3 and wrapped things up but it was a warning shot to Team GB.

Belgium posed little problem as Team GB made it three wins from three matches with a 3-0 scoreline. Ashleigh Ball, Cullen and Laura Bartlett were all on target. Even more heartening was the sight of Kate Walsh on the bench after a three-night stay in hospital, determined to play her part, even with a metal plate in her jaw and a face mask holding her jawbone in place.

This was an unexpected bonus to the side, especially for Walsh, who had been told not to expect a return to the action. Later, it was revealed that the player had been told this so that she would go to surgery in a relaxed state – if she had thought there was any chance of playing again, her body would have been tense and the surgery might not have worked. Even so, Sarah Thomas recalls how the squad were told by Kerry not to stare at Walsh's face when she returned. 'It was a bit odd,' says Thomas. 'There was Kate looking like the Elephant Man and we had to say "Hi Kate, you're looking well."

'We had to watch her sip on protein drinks while we were all eating, and she had to have these painkilling injections before each game, that wore off well before the end of the match. She is an awesome woman.'

The next two matches saw Team GB's smooth progress come to an abrupt halt: a 2-1 loss to China, with a sole goal from Cullen; then a 2-1 loss to the Dutch, again with only Cullen on target for Team GB, meant that Danny Kerry's preparations for the semi-finals would now be all about countering the threat of Argentina and their superstar attacker Luciana Aymar, a player who at that stage had won seven of her eight career World Player of the Year titles.

Commentating on the Games for the BBC, former Great Britain international and Olympian Mel Clewlow said: 'GB won't be happy with three wins and two defeats from their group games. After losing to the Dutch, Danny Kerry was furious – and rightly so. They've lost two pool games and it's only thanks to Japan beating China that they're into the semi-finals. I think they started the tournament really well and I thought this was one of the best British sides I've ever seen, but over the last two games they seem to have lost their way a bit. They're not creating as many chances as they did in the first three games and, at the moment, Crista Cullen is the only one putting the ball in the back of the net from penalty corners.

'When you get to the semi-finals, the big teams work out your strengths and obviously penalty corners is one of them for GB. Argentina will be looking to not give Crista that opportunity.'

And in the end, Clewlow's words rang true. The game came down to some moments of sheer brilliance from Aymar, a stunning goal from Carla Rebecchi, an interpretation of the rules that was questioned by Team GB and a golden opportunity to equalise in the dying moments from one of the least likely people to miss a goalscoring chance, Helen Richardson.

Emma John, writing in *The Guardian*, captured the moments after the final whistle.

" _____

As the whistle blew at the end of Britain's semi-final against Argentina, the pitch looked like a call to prayer. Every single one of the GB players fell to their knees, their heads cast down, each one alone in their grief. They had given their all but finished on the wrong end of a 2-1 scoreline. Instead of appearing in their first Olympic final on Friday, it is Argentina who will play the Netherlands for gold, and Britain will now face New Zealand in a play-off for bronze.

The defeat was made harder by the fact that an obvious infringement preceding Argentina's second goal had been ignored by the umpire. Britain were obstructed in the field before Carla Rebecchi made her bolt to the goalmouth and manoeuvred the ball skilfully around the keeper Beth Storry. But their animated calls for a TV referral were rejected because it had occurred outside of the 23m line.

Speaking after the match with a catch in his voice, Danny Kerry, the British coach, said that the issue had been raised in technical meetings before the tournament. 'We were assured that common sense would prevail,' he said. 'But it hasn't.

'Everyone knew (about the obstruction), the millions on TV, 16,000 in the crowd, 22 players on the pitch, everyone. But unfortunately the law as it is written meant it couldn't be referred. And it's a shame, because it's one of our biggest nights for our sport.

"_____

Netherlands captain Maartje Paumen pumps her fist in delight during her side's 2-1 Pool A triumph against Team GB.
Koen Suyk

Kate Walsh jumps for joy as her side defeat New Zealand in the bronze medal match.
Frank Uijlenbroek

For Beth Storry, it was one of the defining moments of the game. 'There are so many good memories, but the very real disappointment of not winning the semi-final versus Argentina, well that moment and the huge feeling of disappointment still hasn't left, five years on.'

'When the whistle went, I just burst into tears,' says Thomas. 'We had to walk around saying "thank you" to the crowd, I remember Crista had her arm around my shoulder consoling me, but that's all I remember. The next day, the front page of *The Metro* had this image of me crying and Crista hugging me and the headline was "Don't Cry for Me Argentina". We had bought into the vision of gold so much, we totally believed that we could win that medal.

'That night, my room-mate Laura Bartlett and me were watching a DVD that I had been given by Janneke Schopman (Netherlands international and current Team USA coach) because we didn't think we would sleep. It was a comedy and after about three quarters of an hour we laughed at something. I remember we just looked at each other and said, "Oh right, so we can still laugh".'

And so Team GB found themselves fighting for a bronze medal rather than contesting gold against the Netherlands. It would take a superhuman effort to lift themselves up to the challenge. But, said captain Kate, with her jaw bandaged and sporting a face mask, 'Believe you me, we will get up for that bronze medal game.'

It was the same message that the captain had shared with a shattered Sarah Thomas earlier. 'I just remember walking back to the village with Kate that night,' recalls Thomas. 'And we both promised each other solemnly that we would win the bronze. It sounds daft now, but because we had said it to each other, I just knew that Kate would keep that promise and so would I.'

Team GB's opponents in the bronze medal match were New Zealand's Black Sticks. The Oceania team had enjoyed a good Games, with wins against Belgium, USA and South Africa and a draw with Germany. They had a strong, speedy squad and were already on course for a highest ever finish in the Olympics: A bronze would be the icing on the cake.

But a Team GB side determined to bounce back after the disappointment of the semi-finals awaited the Black Sticks.

'I knew going into the bronze medal match that we would come out on top,' says Beth Storry. 'Everyone was on it, there was a buzz in the team and a real focus.'

Sarah Thomas agrees: 'We turned up at the stadium and it was strange, but we had gone from the darkest, dirtiest memory of losing, to this day where the sun was shining and the birds were singing. We rolled up to the pitch and it sounds odd now, but I remember stepping over the sideline and thinking "this is probably my last ever game of hockey and we are going to win today." I never once thought we would lose.'

The match itself saw a patient Team GB side sit out a goal-less first half, with New Zealand creating more openings than the home side. New Zealand then caused a hush in the stadium when Katie Glynn's penalty corner struck the post and rattled away, but that seemed to galvanise Team GB. Alex Danson scored the breakthrough goal, a deflection from a penalty corner. The crowd erupted and the players could sense the atmosphere get thick with expectation. Crista Cullen made it 2-0 as she scored a trademark penalty corner before Sarah Thomas made it 3-0 with another expertly converted penalty corner routine.

There was a consolation goal for the Black Sticks but a rampant Team GB, cheered on by a euphoric partisan crowd of 16,000 people, swept to their first medal at an Olympic Games since Barcelona 1992, where Jane Sixsmith had inspired the team to bronze.

In an interview with the BBC, Team GB captain Kate Walsh said: 'We were heartbroken after our semi-final. The team was devastated, people couldn't talk, they were absolutely gutted.

'Everything we dreamed of was that gold medal. We knew we couldn't get it, but we vowed that we weren't going to go home empty-handed. We knew that we had the game, we knew that we had the mental capacity. We just had to put it all together.'

At a press conference the next morning, a tired but elated Walsh told the gathered press that the past three years had been the most amazing years of her life. 'We made a tough decision in 2009 to say to the world, "This is what we are about" and we have lived that and dragged others with us.

'And just before we went out today, we looked each other in the eye and knew we would do it. It was so special, that moment, I can't describe it and only we know what that feels like.'

While she didn't say it, many present believed that this would be Kate's swansong. The emotional investment of a 13-year international career – most of it as captain – would surely be enough, even for the tough Mancunian?

'You never know what a player is feeling and how much energy they have left to give,' says Storry. 'With Kate, I think that it was good that she had a bit of a break to really come back full of energy and ready to go. Did it surprise me that she continued? No, not really, as I think that she always believed and dreamt of the gold and didn't want to stop before achieving it.'

For Storry though, there was never any plan to go through another four years. The goalkeeper was more than certain that there were players coming through who would fill her kickers. 'Maddie (Hinch) has always been an excellent goalkeeper and pre-London she

Hugs all round as Team GB win their first Olympic hockey medal for 20 years.
Frank Uijlenbroek

was part of our training squad, fighting for her place at London, so it was always evident that there would be no problem filling the void once I'd retired.'

Another player announcing her retirement post-London was Crista Cullen. The joint top scorer at London decided to follow her heart and return to Kenya to help with the family business and 'play a bit of social hockey on the grass pitches'.

'After London and the bronze medal I thought that was as good as it gets. My home and my heart is in Africa and I thought it was time to get on with a career and a life outside of hockey. People watch the Olympics and they don't see the amount of training and demand on an athlete in between a four-year cycle. I couldn't see the wood for the trees as I viewed another four years.'

For Danny Kerry, London 2012 left him, in his words, 'absolutely fried'. Much of this was due to the break to Kate Walsh's jaw early in the tournament. 'I had to spend an incredibly large amount of energy managing and leading that situation with athletes and staff over an extended number of days, which in a home Olympics was already an enormous task.'

The coach spent the day after the bronze medal match sitting in the Olympic stadium watching the men in their bronze medal match (they lost to Australia). This was his opportunity to take in the amazing atmosphere at the Riverbank Arena and just think about the previous two weeks. 'I needed the chance to assimilate what had gone on, but I have to admit my over-riding emotion was one of sheer fatigue.'

Looking back on the 2012 experience, many hockey commentators have said that this was the best GB side ever. For those athletes, a gold medal was very much on the table and the preparations were all geared towards that goal. 'People talk about the preparations that went into Rio, but we were prepared to the same level of detail for London,' says Sarah Thomas. 'We had the training that is now called 'thinking Thursday'; we had the social media ban; we went through extensive media training to deal with the unexpected questions the press might ask. My individual example is that we were doing an interview and someone asked how I would feel as a Welsh person singing the national anthem. It was those questions that could trip you up. We were as prepared for London as it was possible to be.

'I honestly think it just wasn't our time in London. Little things make the difference. Nothing could have prepared us for losing Kate in the first game. We had planned for just about every scenario, but losing your captain was one we had never considered. Winning and losing is all about fine margins and a little bit of luck. But I believe we won in Rio because of the foundations that were set in place in 2009 and nearly came to fruition in 2012.'

For coach Kerry, London hadn't delivered exactly what he wanted but it was another step along the road. 'I'm just really content, that's how I feel,' said Kerry. 'In 2008, I was the classic coach who thought it was all about understanding hockey better than the opposition's coach, and I completely and utterly ignored the most important asset which is your players and your staff.

'You tend to hear about technique, tactics, training hard. The reality is the people who win medals, it comes down to character.'

For the next four years, the character of the team would be tested to the max as Team GB women continued their quest to secure that first ever Olympic gold medal.

Chapter 3

World Cup Misery for England

'There are six countries that think they might have a chance of winning it and we're in that group for sure,' said Jason Lee ahead of the 2014 Rabobank Hockey World Cup.

The World Cup – along with the Olympic Games – is one of the blue riband events in the hockey calendar. The 2014 event took place in the Dutch coastal city of The Hague and was supposed to be a chance for head coach, Jason Lee, and his players to show just how the England team had built on the success enjoyed by Team GB at London 2012. Along with the Commonwealth Games and the European Championships, the World Cup is contested by the home nations, playing in their own right. With the majority of the Great Britain side comprising English players, it came as little surprise that England were seen by many as frontrunners for World Cup glory.

Jason Lee had taken over the women's head coach role in 2013, when Danny Kerry was appointed director of performance – a role that saw Kerry overseeing both the men's and women's elite teams. The appointments reflected Kerry's success in leading the Team GB women to a first Olympic medal since 1992 and a belief on the part of England Hockey that Jason Lee could enhance the progress that Kerry and his staff had already achieved. The coaching staff maintained some consistency in the presence of Karen Brown and John Hurst – assistant coach and manager respectively – but also had some fresh ideas in the shape of Australian goalscoring specialist Craig Keegan and strength and conditioning coach Ben Rosenblatt. Craig Parnham and the previous strength and conditioning coach David Hamilton had both moved to the States to take over as head coach and head of fitness of the ambitious USA women's hockey team.

Renowned for his tactical awareness and innovative ideas for group cohesion and teamwork, Lee was hailed by many, including England and Great Britain assistant coach Karen Brown, as 'one of the most intelligent coaches in the game.'

Like Kerry, Lee was a graduate from Loughborough University. He represented England and Great Britain as an athlete prior to his coaching career – he made his international debut for England at 19 and competed for Team GB at the Barcelona 1992 and Atlanta 1996 Olympic Games.

He retired from playing after the 1998 World Cup in Utrecht and embarked on a coaching career with Loughborough Students and England. He was just 34 years old when he coached Team GB men at Athens 2004, making him one of the youngest national coaches in any British sport.

As men's head coach, Lee's England team won a first ever European title at the 2009 EuroHockey Championships, beating Germany to the gold medal at the event in Amsterdam. He also oversaw a period of improvement for Great Britain men at the Olympic Games, with a ninth place finish at Athens 2004 being followed by fifth at Beijing 2008 and fourth at London 2012, GB's highest finish since their famous gold medal triumph at Seoul 1988.

Lee took over as women's head coach following the London 2012 Olympic Games, and guided England to a silver medal at the EuroHockey Championships in 2013, as well as a bronze medal at the FIH Hockey World League Finals the same year. The previous round of the World League – known as the Semi-Final stage – was a qualifying event for the 2014 World Cup and, at this earlier event held in London, England had secured their passage to The Hague. The team had finished in silver position in London, losing 3-0 to Australia in the final.

Going into the World Cup on the back of a run of successful events, the England team were among the early favourites to at least win a medal, if not take the top spot.

There was undoubtedly a buzz about England's prospects at the World Cup. The communications team back at England Hockey's headquarters at Bisham Abbey was creating positive waves as support was drummed up for the men's and women's squads as they prepared for the competition. And all the players and coaching staff were doing their bit by presenting a positive and united front, in public at least.

An upbeat Jason Lee, speaking to the BBC ahead of the event, said: 'We've beaten both Argentina and Holland in penalty shootouts in the last 12 months by keeping it tight and taking it to penalties.

'We know we've got to be a team that are tough to beat,' he added.

But, behind the scenes, things were far from perfect. Craig Keegan was one year into his role as assistant coach to the squad and he recalls the days leading

Jason Lee, a coach with a lot on his mind.
Frank Uijlenbroek

Former assistant coach to England and Great Britain, Craig Parnham.
Frank Uijlenbroek

Susannah Townsend and Karen Brown watch as England lose to the USA in the opening game of the Rabobank Hockey World Cup 2014.
Frank Uijlenbroek

up to the World Cup: 'It was evident before the World Cup that things weren't right within the group. We had a trip to Germany a couple of months before and we had a number of team meetings during that week. Some issues arose that set the alarm bells ringing.

'Some of those were as a result of leadership, or lack of it, at the time and others were the result of interpersonal issues within the playing group.

'We didn't do enough about that before the World Cup. We didn't do as much to address it as we should have done or could have done. So it was left as "Oh dear, we are not going to have a very good World Cup" and instead of sitting down and addressing those issues, it was just left to fester a bit.'

Kate Richardson-Walsh agrees with Keegan. 'We weren't performing in the build-up (in 2014) and off the pitch there was the culture where cracks can appear in the squad. It's perhaps what we saw under a massive microscope at the World Cup. We believed we could medal. We capitulated and it was devastating.'

England's growing problems aside, the World Cup was a glorious festival of hockey. The Hague is one of the hot spots of hockey in the Netherlands, a fact proven by their decision to temporarily convert the 15,000 capacity Kyocera Stadium, home of football team ADO Den Haag, into one of the finest hockey arenas in the world. The hockey obsession wasn't confined to just the venue either. Beach hockey and street hockey tournaments were taking place throughout the city, while down the road in Rotterdam a fiercely contested Masters World Cup was running parallel to the main event.

The Hockey Village at the stadium was a daily buzz of hockey enthusiasm. Stalls selling every brand of hockey equipment and clothing; a huge food village serving all manner of ethnic foods; juice bars, coffee

bars, beer tents; a healthy eating stand; and hockey-related activities drew spectators to the ground early and kept them there for hours after the action finished. Players and officials were dropped at the edge of the Hockey Village for their matches and picked up from the same spot. Before and after every game the players had to make their way through the spectators. Following a win, the players happily stopped to greet family and friends and sign autographs for adoring fans; following a defeat, the return to the team bus felt like a walk of shame.

The opening game was against the 11th ranked team, the USA. There was an added frisson to the match as the head coach on the other bench was Craig Parnham and sitting alongside him was former Great Britain fitness coach David Hamilton. If anyone knew where England's weaknesses lay and how to exploit these weaknesses, it would be Parnham and Hamilton.

Looking back on that time, Parnham says that his knowledge of the England squad was undeniably helpful in preparing his players to take on a team that was eight places higher in the world rankings. 'A knowledge of individual players' tendencies can help anticipate situations that may present themselves, though sometimes the detail can become overwhelming. It was more important for our players to understand their own roles.' As the USA tore into the England defence, it was clear that Parnham had primed his team well.

It was the worst possible of starts for England. Paige Selenski's pin-point penalty corner in the third minute gave USA the lead and just 13 minutes later, Kelsey Kolojejchick doubled the lead, again through a corner. England fought back and Kate Richardson-Walsh scored from a penalty corner in the 56th minute,

Kate Richardson-Walsh contemplates a 3-0 loss to China.
Frank Uijlenbroek

but there was no way back against the energetic and inspired USA side.

'The game was close throughout, with England creating chances in both halves,' says Parnham. 'But we were happy with the way we were playing. Our corners were good and were causing problems. I had great confidence in our team but there was a sense of relief at the final whistle, we knew the importance of starting well in a tournament like the World Cup. Momentum is a powerful force in sport. It's best to have it with you.'

Unfortunately for England, momentum was just one of many factors that was missing. Speaking after that opening game, Lee remained upbeat. 'I think it focusses our minds a bit more,' he said. 'Fundamentally we didn't start well and they took two well-worked corners.'

If that match was a setback, the next game was a nightmare. A 3-0 loss to China saw the team start a slow but inevitable implosion. England had more than 25 attempts on goal: China had three.

An emotional Kate Richardson-Walsh spoke after the game: 'We prepared professionally, as we always do, and did our homework on the opposition. I'm just devastated. There are still a lot of games to go in the tournament but one thing we pride ourselves on is our fight and we've been lacking a bit of that.

'We need to be hard and honest with each other and come out for the rest of this tournament and play like an England team play.'

Craig Keegan echoed Parnham's sentiments about momentum and its importance. For the assistant coach, the World Cup was one of those occasions when momentum and luck took over, aided and abetted by the ugly mood in the England camp. 'Once you have a couple of results that don't go your way then momentum is lost. Momentum was very much against us in The Hague and it continued because of the way we were.

'The World Cup could have been so very different, even with all those issues. The first couple of games, we had the better of both matches for at least three-quarters of them. Against the USA we statistically beat them, but we didn't score goals and against China, we had four times the number of shots to them and lost 3-0.'

The next opponents were South Africa. The African champions came to the event ranked 12th in the world and neither England nor Great Britain had lost to them in a major competition since the African nation's reintroduction onto the international stage following the end of apartheid. A 4-1 mauling was the last thing anyone expected and a visibly shocked English team trooped off the pitch, knowing that they would definitely not be contesting any of the top spots.

For midfielder Georgie Twigg, this was the lowest point of the entire World Cup experience: 'In that game against South Africa, we just didn't play anything like the team that we knew we were, the complete opposite in fact. Everyone wanted to do something individually, it was just chaos. I remember being totally exhausted because we had no structure and it was just end-to-end. It was truly, truly awful.'

By now even Lee's positivity had seeped away: 'It's as bad as it gets. We're going to finish the tournament a long way from our potential and our ranking.

'This is rock bottom. As a player and coach this is my fifth World Cup and this is the worst of those experiences, that's for sure.'

The final two pool games were a case of restricting damage. First they faced Argentina, ranked at number two in the world and with a host of star players that included the multiple World Player of the Year, Luciana Aymar, this was a fixture that a damaged England could have done without.

As it turned out, England put in a much improved performance, taking the lead through Alex Danson just seven minutes into the game. As hopes of a good result began to build, Argentina not only struck back through Delfina Merino but they turned the screw when Carla Rebecchi scored from a penalty corner in the final seconds to take the match 2-1. Georgie Twigg, whose foul led to that crucial penalty corner goal, left the pitch inconsolable.

'It was awful,' says the midfielder, who still shudders as she recalls that time. 'The morale was low, confidence was shattered, we felt isolated and no-one knew how to resolve anything. It is so hard during a tournament to resolve things because the games just come one after the other. We just wanted it to all be over so we could go home and regroup.'

Somehow, England got their mojo back for the final pool match against Germany, another team who had not enjoyed a good World Cup. A match that started quietly burst into life in the second half when four goals were scored within an 11-minute spell. The result, 3-1 to England, could not prevent a bottom place finish in the pool, but it did give the players a lift before their final game.

For that game to be an 11th-place play-off against Belgium, the lowest ranked team in the competition, was so far removed from the team's initial hopes and ambitions that it was clear that the writing was on the wall for Jason Lee and his team.

The final match did little to placate a hostile English press. The team worked

South Africa celebrate after an unexpected 4-1 victory over England.
Frank Uijlenbroek

hard against Belgium, but it was a dour, uninspiring performance. England took an early lead but Belgium scored in the final minute of play to send the match to shootout. With a glimpse into a brighter future, Maddie Hinch saved four of the five Belgian shootout efforts and England claimed victory, but there was little in the way of celebration.

Lee maintained an inscrutable composure in front of the media but behind the scenes it was anything but calm. The team left The Hague promptly and returned to Bisham Abbey to face the inevitable fall-out.

'What we heard in the debrief was brutal,' says England Hockey's chief executive, Sally Munday. 'It wasn't just the players, we had everyone in, coaches, back-up staff, we had to get to the bottom of what had gone wrong. There were tears, there was anger, there was recrimination but we had to go through that procedure. We had to go to the deepest, darkest depths before we could start to build again.'

Looking back, Craig Keegan says that the World Cup experience was the 'perfect storm of interplaying factors'.

'Jason (Lee) had a certain style – he is an outstanding coach – and I think what he was trying to do was exactly right but he was trying to do it a bit quickly. He was trying to generate more leaders within the group and trying to give younger players leadership experience. It was just a bit too drastic to change at the time.

'There were also selection issues and some of the players were open about the fact they didn't agree with some selections.

'And, the preparation wasn't anywhere near good enough either. You can roll all those things together and come out with a bit of a storm. It wasn't down to one thing and there isn't one individual to blame.'

While the issues behind England's capitulation were complex, there is little doubt that among the contributory factors to England's poor performances in The Hague is the absence of one of its key performers.

Helen Richardson-Walsh had endured an eight-week-long battle with the treadmill to get back to fitness after a career-saving back operation. Her endeavours were charted through an inspirational blog 'Back to my Best', where she outlined her fight to return to match fitness.

Keep my head up; keep my heart strong

Extract from 'Back to my Best'

"

Whenever I go on twitter I will often see one of the International Hockey Federation tweets counting down the days to the World Cup. The excitement for the tournament is building, but in all honesty whenever I catch a glimpse of it I get a sickening tug in the pit of my stomach.

Today's countdown says there's 40 days to go which is still a great deal of time for me to make huge strides forward. That's just less than six weeks away, and with how things are going, I really believe I can be fit in time to be at the World Cup though I need to get selected into the team; and that date comes much sooner. Every day I tell myself to keep fighting and put myself in the strongest position possible, ignoring that feeling in my stomach as much as I can.

I've had one hell of a week: it's seen me go from just starting to run, to doing hockey-running sessions, 1 v

Germany and England: two teams on the search for form.
Frank Uijlenbroek.

Alex Danson in full flight in the 11/12 play-off against Belgium.
Frank Uijlenbroek

1s and sprinting on the treadmill at altitude. The hockey-running sessions involve different types of movement you'd expect to see on the pitch like tackling, passing and dribbling which were interspersed with the hard yards including accelerations and decelerations, which is the thing that really takes it out of you. It felt so good to get a stick in my hand and instead of any chocolate eggs this year, my gift on Easter Sunday was to do some 1 v 1s.

I've also completed four killer running sessions and two hideous bike sessions at an altitude of 3,000m: the equivalent of a third of the way up Mt. Everest. We are very lucky to have a chamber at Bisham Abbey and the resident EIS (English Institute of Sport) physiologist Luke Gupta, has kindly agreed to oversee my intense two-week programme which will hopefully speed up my adaptation and accelerate my fitness, so when I get back onto the pitch I'll be better able to cope.

,,

Captain Kate marshalling her troops against Belgium.
Frank Uijlenbroek

History will recall that, despite some Herculean efforts, Helen didn't make the squad. In a moving interview in *The Daily Express* with the late Graham Wilson, she said: 'Since finding out I can no longer realise my dream of becoming a world champion, I feel like I've experienced every emotion under the sun.

'I have lost the chance to achieve a goal of mine that not only have I worked incredibly hard for over these last 11 weeks, but completely dedicated my life to for the past 15 years. I have no idea when I will get to the acceptance stage. I keep fluxing between the anger, bargaining and depression stages (of the grief cycle).'

Instead of taking to the pitch alongside wife Kate Richardson-Walsh, Helen commentated on the action from the comfort of the Sky Sports studio instead, but the impact of her absence cannot be underestimated.

Sophie Bray celebrates.
Frank Uijlenbroek.

Speaking to *The Daily Telegraph* just days before the World Cup began, Kate Richardson-Walsh revealed just how hard she was finding it to be captaining a side that did not have her wife's name on the team sheet.

'I kept on refreshing my emails. When it arrived I scanned for her name and it wasn't there.

'She'd got herself back playing and because there was a month to go, with her experience and what she brings to the team - I am biased - I would have had her in the squad.'

The decision by the selectors not to take Helen to the World Cup had an undoubted impact upon Kate and, as she admits, created tension within an already fractured squad.

'As captain you stand in the middle. I felt in my career that you should stand at that midpoint, absolutely to be there for the players but also to understand the needs of the coach.

'That leads to many arguments with the players, so this is the first time where I went more down the scale of the player, purely and simply because it was my wife. I felt that it was important to care for my wife at that point, as she was going through a horrible, emotional time and she needed my support more than anything.

'I just took my captain's hat off for a week or so. Some might say that's not professional but in my opinion that was the best thing to do.

'If she wasn't my wife or friend I would still say she is one of the best players in the world,' added Kate. 'What she brings on to the pitch is world class, but it is the little conversations, the boost she gives the team when she gets subbed on, it picks everybody up.'

Just how much an almost fit Helen Richardson-Walsh would have added to the side that travelled to The Hague is debatable, but what would Lee have given for a boost to the team as they went into free-fall?

The fall-out for Kate Richardson-Walsh continued after the World Cup had ended. Already considering retirement before the World Cup, it now seemed inevitable that the England and Great Britain captain would take her leave from the sport, in a manner far from how she would have chosen or imagined.

Kate took herself away from the spotlight for several weeks, travelling the world and coaching hockey in Hong Kong and Japan.

'I just needed a break. I found myself asking the question "Do you love it, or not?" It was mental more than anything else. I was finding it very difficult. So I decided

Maddie Hinch prepares for the shootout against Belgium.
Frank Uijlenbroek

I needed some time away to think about it properly. And that time and space gave me the realisation that I wasn't done with it, that I was motivated. I realised that there was still a lot I wanted to do and achieve and I wanted to fight for my place again.'

On reflection, those torrid days in The Hague may well have provided the platform for success in Rio. Certainly, it is a viewpoint to which most of the team now subscribe. 'The conversations that took place afterwards were so tough,' says Georgie Twigg. 'We really examined the nitty gritty and there were a lot of tears. But everything that has happened as a result, how we learnt from that experience, well that has been fantastic.

'As a team, by the time we got to Rio we were as close-knit as it is possible to get. We all had each others' backs and we were making decisions together, that is a very powerful thing.'

From 2013 until the World Cup, Danny Kerry had been working for England Hockey as performance director. In that position, he would have full insight into Lee's thinking and strategy. Looking back at that time, Kerry is both sympathetic and admiring of his coaching colleague. 'Jason Lee set things in place that were fantastic,' says Kerry. 'I think some of the ideas, he just

tried to implement too quickly. I think some of Jason's thinking was in the right direction. Unfortunately, for whatever reason, the players didn't go with him. His fault wasn't tactics or strategy, it was failing to get his players to work with him.'

The 2014 World Cup – the nightmare by numbers

Pool Matches:
England v USA 1-2 *(Kate Richardson-Walsh)*
England v China 0-3
England v South Africa 1-4 *(Nicola White)*
England v Argentina 1-2 *(Alex Danson)*
England v Germany 3-1 *(Hannah Macleod, Susie Gilbert, Susannah Townsend)*

11th/12th play-off
England v Belgium 1-1 *(2-1 after shootout) (Sophie Bray)*

Chapter 4

The Rollercoaster Years

When England left The Hague after the debacle of the 2014 World Cup, it was to return to a debrief that was 'brutal' and left some of the players at their lowest ebb.

In an interview with *The Telegraph* newspaper on 10 June 2014, Danny Kerry, in his role as performance director for Great Britain and England Hockey said: 'I guess you have to ask whether it is a systemic or situational thing. We won't know until we have scratched the surface. We have had a successful 2013 and a disappointing World Cup.'

Both Kerry and head coach Jason Lee referred to 'complex issues' that had been at the heart of the four opening defeats at the World Cup, with Kerry saying 'painful questions' would be asked on the squad's return to the UK. 'If it was a simple answer I would give it to you,' he said to the gallery of journalists at the final press conference in The Hague.

Jason Lee left almost immediately, while the squad and the remainder of the coaching team set about unearthing what had gone wrong and, importantly, what they were going to do about it.

The chief executive officer at England Hockey, Sally Munday, winces as she recalls that time.

> *There were a lot of tears, there were a lot of very honest words spoken and I don't think it is an exaggeration to say that some of the players were left feeling emotionally extremely raw. And to recover from that takes a long time and is a slow healing process. But, it was an important part of their recovery. They had to hit those lows to really know how to win.*

One of the first stages in the recovery process was controversial. Danny Kerry was reinstated as head coach, while maintaining his overall role as performance director. This was a decision that caused *The Telegraph*'s hockey writer Rod Gilmour to ask: 'The current scenario does sound confusing; one wonders whether England Hockey ever look further afield, given that Kerry and Lee have handled both women's and men's roles in the past.'

Gilmour and others among the British press were concerned that, as director of performance, Kerry was the person responsible for managing the head coach. In other words, who would now assess Kerry's performance?

To the beleaguered players this was the least of their worries. With his track record of a bronze medal at

Sam Quek focuses as England prepare to face China for fifth place at the 2014 Champions Trophy in Mendoza, Argentina.
Frank Uijlenbroek

Alex Danson defying gravity at the EuroHockey Championships 2015.
Koen Suyk

Team GB celebrate in Valencia as they win the 2015 Hockey World League Semi-Final and secure qualification for Rio 2016.
Frank Uijlenbroek

Danny Kerry and Alex Danson discuss tactics at the Champions Trophy, Mendoza 2014.
Frank Uijlenbroek

London 2012 and his ability to unite the players, in chief executive Sally Munday's eyes, Kerry was the man for the job: 'It is notoriously difficult to appoint top coaches mid-cycle as the best coaches are usually contracted and committed for an Olympic cycle.

'As part of the recruitment process we spoke to a number of coaches at home and abroad but simply could not get the right person. It was suggested by someone that Danny could go back into the role.

'He is an exceptional coach, his planning and attention to detail is superb and he recognises that it is much more than just hockey that makes a winning team. What is done away from the pitch has as much importance to him and you could see that in the culture of the group. Danny is also totally committed to making himself better. He is always looking at what he can learn and who he can learn from; his thirst for knowledge and self-improvement is key to his success.'

With the coaching dilemma resolved, it was time to get the team's progress to Rio back on track, although the size of the mountain left to climb looked a daunting challenge. If the public and the hockey press were both bemused at England's capitulation in The Hague, the players were no less so. Georgie Twigg looks back with genuine bewilderment: 'It is difficult to explain,' she says. 'I think it was an accumulation of things not quite going right at the time and it all just came to a head at the World Cup. It was awful, truly awful, that tournament. We were not quite sure how to resolve it and everyone became quite isolated.

'Once a team's morale is down it can become difficult, and our confidence was completely shattered. It is hard to resolve that in a tournament because it is so

fast paced, you are quickly onto the next game. We all just wanted it to end. We literally just wanted it to end.'

Of course, the problems didn't cease when the team arrived back at Bisham Abbey. 'We had a lot of meetings when we got back from The Hague, and they were not nice,' says Twigg. 'There were a lot of tears – it was very emotional at times. But, we needed to have those to allow ourselves to move forward and grow.'

Kerry himself was realistic about the task ahead: 'We have a hell of a long way to go if we aspire to become a world top three side again. What fills me with motivation, however, is that we can travel a long way in a short space of time.'

The first major challenge faced by the England team was the Commonwealth Games in Glasgow. England had won medals on six consecutive occasions at the Commonwealth Games, but they had never won gold. Top of the podium here would go some way towards erasing the pain of the World Cup. Coming just a month after their haranguing in The Hague, the question was whether the players had enough self-belief to shut up the doubters and play to their potential?

The answer was 'yes', but with some reservations. They beat Wales, Malaysia and Scotland to take second place in the pool but, the opening match against Wales was anything but comprehensive, and Scotland – inspired by the brilliance of Team GB star and London 2012 bronze medallist Emily Maguire – put the England team under enormous physical pressure through which they battled to a 2-1 win. This would not be the first time that Danny Kerry spoke about his acceptance that sometimes the team had to 'win ugly'.

A pool stage loss to Australia meant they met New Zealand in the semi-finals. The Black Sticks had breezed unbeaten through the pool stages, scoring 25 goals and conceding just one. But, while New Zealand have a great record of reaching semi-finals, they do have one weak spot – shootouts – and this semi-final in Glasgow was to prove no different. The match finished 1-1 and the teams prepared for the shootout. It gave Maddie Hinch the chance to show her extraordinary ability in these pressured situations and, with two saves to her name, she led England to victory and a chance to contest a first ever Commonwealth gold medal.

The final itself made for agonising viewing if you were an England fan. England were 1-0 up against Australia, courtesy of 19-year-old rising star Lily Owsley, but rather than pressing home the advantage, they retreated into a backs-to-the-wall defence. With just 11 seconds left, Jodie Kenny struck home a penalty corner to take the game to a shootout. Even Hinch was powerless to deny the Hockeyroos their fourth Commonwealth gold medal.

'We were defending a lot and stopped trying to play hockey,' Kerry recalls. 'Australia were pressing up high and we didn't have that level of experience to continue to play. The pressure built and built.

'I was gutted but philosophical,' he says of the defeat. 'Australia were the best team at the tournament but to nearly sneak it was testimony to the application of the girls. Had we snuck it just by defending, I would have been happy to have won, but equally Australia was the better team over the tournament.'

Next stop for the England team was the Champions Trophy in Mendoza where they were in a pool alongside Australia, Germany and the host nation, Argentina. It was an event where the matches played second fiddle to one player, the eight-time World Player of the Year Luciana Aymar. This was to be Aymar's final fling and, every time Argentina played, the stands were crammed with vociferous, blue-and-white-clad fans watching the swansong of one of hockey's greatest ever players.

Helen Richardson-Walsh, still out of the game as she continued to recover from surgery, spoke about the Argentine superstar: 'I particularly remember playing against her in the 2010 World Cup hosted by Argentina. It was a memorable tournament for many reasons but to see Aymar being worshipped by the home fans was something else, while her goal celebrations in that tournament were pretty special. I can't imagine any player in Britain getting that sort of reception.'

The team that travelled to Mendoza was significantly different to the team that won silver in Glasgow. Aside from Helen, Kate Richardson-Walsh was still taking time away from the sport and Nicola White failed to make the cut. There were call-ups for Shona McCallin, Joie Leigh and Sarah Haycroft. In addition, prolific striker Alex Danson played only one match before a serious head injury, sustained against Australia, ruled her out of any further action.

England enjoyed mixed results in Mendoza. Australia continued to be a bogey side, nicking a 2-1 win with five minutes to spare in the opening game. This was followed by a 1-1 draw against Germany – a match that German captain Janne Müller-Weiland described as 'more like ping-pong than hockey'. The final pool game was a baptism of fire for some of the players. At eight o'clock at night the temperature in Argentina may have been cooling but the stadium became an inferno when Las Leonas entered the fray.

England adapted well to the pressure and took an early 1-0 lead, but three goals within nine minutes and a fourth to seal the win, saw Argentina march on to the top of the pool. The results meant England would face New Zealand in the quarter-finals.

Alex Danson and Hannah Macleod celebrate England's title success at the EuroHockey Championships 2015.
Frank Uijlenbroek

England become European champions.
Frank Uijlenbroek

The quarter-final in Mendoza saw Kerry's team wilt in the heat as New Zealand proved dominant throughout the match. The 3-1 win was a just result as England laboured to put moves together and New Zealand demonstrated the tough approach they take to their matches. The result meant England faced China for minor honours and left Kerry scratching his head.

'What that experience proved, more than anything,' said the coach reflecting back, 'is just how important it is to train players to last for an entire tournament. It is no good being brilliant for four games and then fading away, you must be able to play back-to-back games and last the duration.'

It was an experience that Kerry digested. Two years later he would select a team that was packed with players who were, in the coach's words, not necessarily the best, but the ones who could last eight matches – pool round to final.

The team left Mendoza in fifth place, but for Kerry and his team, this was not so much a disappointment, as a huge step along the learning curve.

As 2014 drew to a welcome end, Danny Kerry shared his views with England Hockey's communications officer Ross Bone about preparations for the forthcoming Olympic qualification tournament and Rio 2016 itself. 'Penalty corner conversion remains a priority for us, along with a continued focus on open play goalscoring. We will now further focus on aspects of delivering these under pressure and ensuring our daily training environment

recreates the specificity needed for this development.

'I'm looking forward to being able to play regularly as Great Britain from January onwards as we've largely only been able to do this in training during a period where we've predominantly been competing as home nations. The talent across the wider Great Britain squad is an exciting prospect and brings extra competitiveness to selection and raises the bar of performance even further.'

And so to Valencia in June 2015, where the Hockey World League (HWL) Semi-Finals offered the first chance for sides to qualify for the Olympic Games. Under International Hockey Federation (FIH) rules, the teams that finished in the top three in the HWL Semi-Finals would automatically book a berth to Rio 2016. Failure to qualify at this point would mean that Team GB's Olympic qualification hopes would be reliant on England winning the EuroHockey Championships continental qualifier and, with the Netherlands, Germany and Spain all capable of taking the required first-place finish, it was certainly the more difficult route.

'We went to Spain knowing that this was a golden opportunity for us to get the qualification spot,' says Kerry as he reflects back. 'Once that was secured we could concentrate upon our preparations for Rio.'

Things could not have gone better for Kerry and his team. The opening match mirrored the shape of things to come. A 2-0 win over host nation Spain got the party started and this result was followed by pool wins over Argentina (2-0), Canada (4-2) and China (2-0). The quarter-final match was a 2-0 victory over South Africa, which left Team GB facing Germany in the semi-finals.

Whoever won that game was guaranteed a place at Rio 2016, so it was with huge relief that Danny Kerry faced the press after he watched his team grind out a tense 1-0 win. 'For 15 minutes we were awesome. After that we won ugly. That in itself is a quality which we have worked hard to drive into the team. We should have been out of sight with the clear chances we created, but after we didn't take them the game became nervy with so much at stake. Our character showed through and we are now officially Rio-bound.'

On paper the final match was a formality. Both Team GB and their opponents, China, had accomplished what they set out to do, but this was the Team GB team's chance to show that they had bounced back in style. Another 2-0 victory, courtesy of goals from Hollie Webb and Alex Danson, saw the team win seven from seven, with Sophie Bray emerging as joint top goalscorer alongside Argentina's Carla Rebecchi. It seemed that Kerry had found the team capable of seeing a tournament through to the end, however, the coach, normally one for keeping things quiet and calm, unleashed a bombshell when he announced that he was asking Crista Cullen - who had been living in Kenya since 2012 - to rejoin the training squad.

As the defender reveals, this had been part of Kerry's plans for a while.

'Danny phoned me in April 2015,' she recalls. 'I was working, had a full-time job, had a life, had everything back in Kenya and had no intention of returning back to the squad at that stage. I had obviously seen the World Cup results and the European Championships were coming up, so I was taking an avid interest in what was going on, but at no stage did I think I would ever be coming back.

'Then my personal circumstances changed and Danny said that he wanted to give me a window of six months in order to deliberate that decision, within which time the girls had qualified for the Rio Olympics, by going to Valencia and playing very well to win the tournament.

'At that time I thought: "Do you know what Crista, rather than being worried about putting your neck on the block and just risking your pride, to come back and have another shot at an Olympics is a pretty amazing thing to be offered." That said, there were no guarantees for me.'

For someone as meticulous in his planning as Danny Kerry, this appeared an oddly out-of-character decision, which could have gone catastrophically wrong. However, the clue was always there, as Kerry had not been reticent in acknowledging that his team needed someone with the ability to score from penalty

Great Britain face host nation Argentina in the heat of Rosario.
Frank Uijlenbroek

corners, and Cullen was by far the best player available to him on that front. She was also a born leader, a quality that would prove invaluable further down the line.

Cullen acknowledges the risk her coach had taken. 'Yes, it was a complete gamble. I hadn't played hockey in three years, properly, other than the odd Friday evening on a half pitch in Kenya somewhere, which was more as a bit of fun rather than actually playing hockey. All I could control was actually being fit enough. I had to earn my stripes. I had to get myself into the 31-player squad and then try to get myself into the 16, and I had a ten-month window to do that.'

Not only was Cullen's match readiness in question, there was the potential impact that including a player who had not been part of the squad for nearly three years would have on the other athletes, particularly those whose place was under threat.

Cullen set about dealing with the issues in her own forthright manner, determined to make it clear to the group that she was returning at Danny's invitation and not because she had decided that, with Rio 2016 on the horizon, the time was right to step back into the fold. 'I said to Danny that this is how it needs to be put across to the group and that, fundamentally, will make a difference to how I am accepted within the group.

'Not only that, I had to have hard conversations with the people I would be directly competing with, which was important. As an experienced player, I took the initiative to have those conversations to say "let the best person get the job". That was the best way I could approach it.

'Thankfully, those athletes accepted me in light of what had happened and we were able to prepare in the best way we possibly could, which is ultimately what we were all trying to achieve.'

Cullen's reinstatement into the squad was backed by captain Kate Richardson-Walsh, who said with her usual honesty: 'Whether Crista gets in the team or makes other players push themselves, it is a positive.

'In the short term that's hard to deal with but in the long term, with sending the best team possible to Rio in mind, it can only be a positive. At the same time, I think naturally as defenders, there is the reaction that "she could take my place".'

Three major tournaments now stood between Great Britain and Rio 2016. The vast majority of the squad would feature for England at the EuroHockey Championships; then it was off to Rosario, Argentina with Great Britain for the Hockey World League Final in December, before a last blast with Great Britain at the Champions Trophy in London in June 2016, just two months before the Opening Ceremony in Rio.

Georgie Twigg consoles Maddie Hinch after a 2-1 loss to New Zealand at the Hockey World League Final 2015 in Rosario, Argentina.
Frank Uijlenbroek

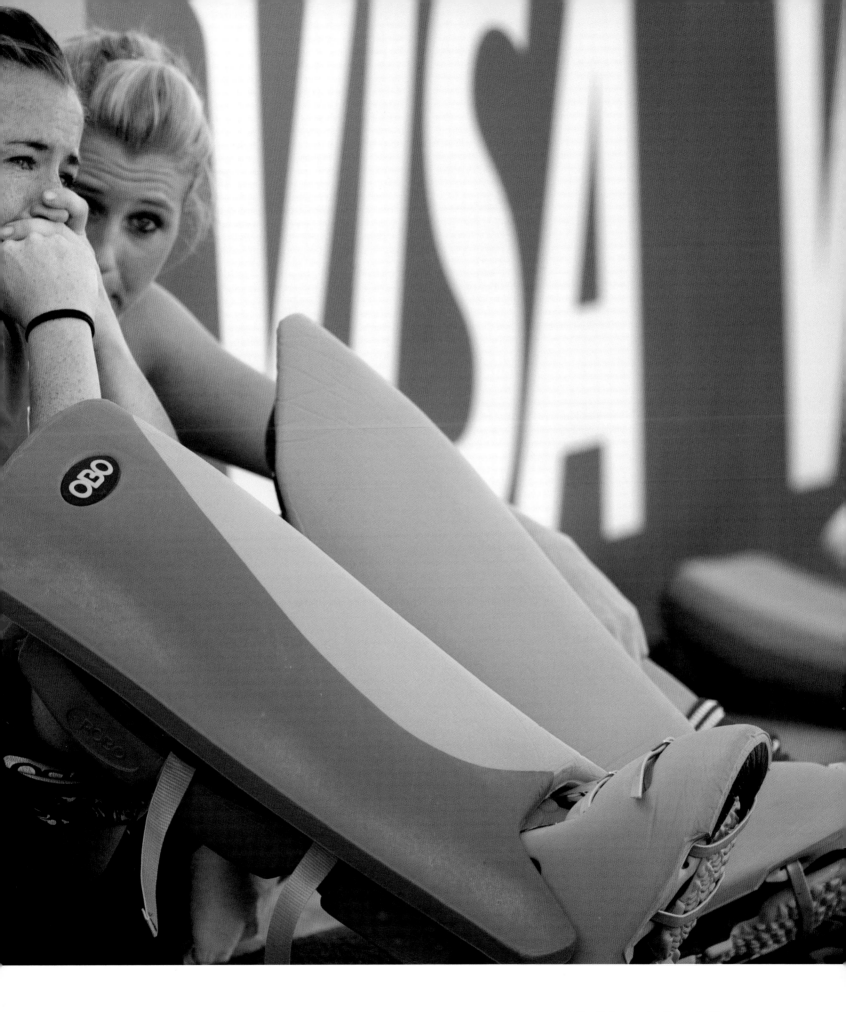

'If you had told me we (GB and England combined) would have a 15-match unbeaten run this year, I would have just laughed,' said a jubilant Danny Kerry after England cruised to gold at the 2015 EuroHockey Championships. Unbeaten in all pool matches, the team faced Spain in the semi-finals and, despite playing a very tense and nervy game, they prevailed 2-1 to set up a match against the world number one side, The Netherlands.

The match went according to the rankings until the final quarter. England had put up a strong resistance but eventually, Dutch guile wore them down and with 10 minutes left the Netherlands had a 2-0 lead.

After the game, Georgie Twigg spoke of the moment the mood on the pitch changed: 'When we went 2-0 down we looked at each other and we knew what we had to do. We don't train day in, day out to go down without a fight. The belief we have is incredible and will take us far in this next year. Once the first goal went in I knew we could do it.'

First Sophie Bray and then Lily Owsley put away penalty corners and at the other end of the pitch, Maddie Hinch made an athletic double save. It took the match into shootout and the largely British crowd at the Lee Valley Hockey & Tennis Centre were in for a treat.

First up was Helen Richardson-Walsh, who was back in the fold and as influential as ever. She was fouled by Joyce Sombroek in the Netherlands goal and took the resultant penalty stroke herself and scored. Hinch consulted her notebook before taking her place between the posts and duly saved from Willemijn Bos to keep it 1-0. Danson kept her cool to slot home the second and Hinch put down her notebook, strolled to the goal and denied Lidewij Welten. Bray converted hers and Ellen Hoog got Netherlands on the board. Sombroek saved Twigg's effort but Hinch had one last check of her notes and Eva de Goede knew she was doomed. England women had won their first European gold medal since 1991 and they were delighted.

And so to Argentina for the Hockey World League Finals. As winners of their Semi-Final round and with the vast majority of the squad on a high following England's win at the EuroHockey Championships, Great Britain were expected to perform well. But as it quickly transpired, this was to be another dip on their rollercoaster journey.

'Unless we go through these experiences, we won't actually be fully prepared for Rio,' said Kerry after he watched his team finish in seventh place, after getting muscled out of the running for a top four

Great Britain's Hollie Webb and Jane Claxton of Australia show full commitment to the cause at the 2016 Champions Trophy in London.
Frank Uijlenbroek

Great expectations as Great Britain face New Zealand at the Hockey World League Final 2015 competition in Rosario, Argentina.
Frank Uijlenbroek

finish by New Zealand in the quarter-finals. Prior to that, Great Britain had put in an underwhelming set of performances, losing to Argentina 2-1, beating an understrength Australia 1-0, and drawing 1-1 with China in desultory fashion. This was as far removed from the heady days of Valencia and London as it was possible to get, and the players looked fatigued and despondent as they left the stadium each day.

As the team retired to lick their wounds, Helen Richardson-Walsh echoed her coach's philosophical approach: 'No team becomes a bad one overnight. Yes, there are some critical things we need to look at and do better with, but this is an amazing squad and the European success shows what we can accomplish when we get it right.'

The final major tournament before the Olympic Games was the 2016 Champions Trophy in London and the stadium was packed every time Great Britain were in action. England's statistics at the EuroHockey Championships a year earlier had read seven wins from seven. Great Britain's stats at the Champions Trophy made poorer reading: six matches, four losses, one draw, one win. That the win was in the final match, a comprehensive 4-1 triumph against New Zealand, made the pill slightly less difficult to swallow, but the home crowd had come to expect magic, and instead they encountered a horror show.

'I'm probably going to get into trouble for saying this, but we have not been good enough here in London. We know that we are capable of producing so much more than this. We all feel the same. We want to go out there and show the world how good we are. We still believe that we can go to Rio and take home the gold – we know we can compete with anyone.'

That was the reaction of a bitterly disappointed Susannah Townsend immediately after Great Britain had

lost their fourth match in succession. For the combative midfielder, the match on Saturday 25 June 2016 was supposed to be the celebration of a personal milestone, her 100th senior international appearance, being played at the same venue where she had become a European champion with England just one year earlier. Instead, she was left dealing with the scrutiny that followed yet another defeat in Great Britain's final competition ahead of the Rio 2016 Olympic Games.

In the lead-up to the Champions Trophy, Townsend herself had described the event as an opportunity for competing teams to build some momentum going into the Olympic Games. Sadly, to the many onlookers it seemed that GB were handing the impetus to their opponents in their own back yard.

The increased concern following this particular result was not simply because the team had lost again. It was the significance of who they had lost to. Their conquerors on the day were Australia, a team they would face just six weeks later in their opening match of the Rio 2016 Olympic Games. The manner of the defeat also raised eyebrows, with the Hockeyroos completely dominating the hosts to cruise to a worryingly comfortable 4-1 triumph. The result condemned Great Britain to the 5-6 classification match, where they would need to beat New Zealand on the final day simply to avoid the ignominy of a last place finish on home soil.

Whilst defeat against the third ranked Australians, the 2014 World Cup silver medallists, was not in itself something to be ashamed of, the sub-standard performance was deemed unacceptable by head coach Danny Kerry and team captain Kate Richardson-Walsh. Both made it clear in no uncertain terms that things needed to change, and fast.

'We had firm words after the game, they were the firmest we have had in a long while,' said Sam Quek, speaking to GB Hockey's media team following the match. 'It shouldn't take the captain or the coach to stand up to speak to us in that manner but I think we needed it today. We need to fight, make those tackles so no one goes through us and we need to show character. The bottom line is that we need to give everyone something to cheer about tomorrow.'

If Saturday's post-game reprimand from the coach and captain was designed to inspire a reaction, it certainly had the desired effect. The patience of the ever-faithful GB fans was finally rewarded when the team produced by far and away their best performance of the competition, battling to a superb 4-3 victory over New Zealand's Black Sticks. A brilliant hat-trick from star striker Alex Danson stole the headlines, but it was the quality of the team display which really caught the eye, showing everyone what these players were capable of when they hit top gear.

Speaking after the match, a grateful Alex Danson thanked all of the fans for their constant support throughout an event that may not have gone to plan, but had ended on a very positive note. 'I don't think anyone has lost faith in us and we haven't lost faith in ourselves,' said Danson, who was quick to also talk about the remarkable unity that had remained within the group despite the results not going their way. 'It was really important to get the win today but even though it has been a difficult week, the one thing that hasn't been lost is that sense of togetherness. We know what we are about, we knew coming into this tournament it could go brilliantly well or not so well but it would have no impact on what we can achieve going into Rio.'

Danson's words were telling. Of course winning the 5-6 classification match was never going to set the world alight. However, the result and, more importantly, the performance served as a timely reminder of the quality and potential contained within this group of players. The post-match media interviews were filled with a renewed sense of optimism, with Danson and her team-mates having the collective demeanour of a group firmly in the belief that they had turned a corner.

'We will go back to Bisham Abbey now, we have a few weeks to consolidate our final preparations,' continued Danson. 'I believe we have the best training programme out there, the best staff and the best players. It is pretty exciting moving into the final period of time before the Olympics. Sometimes a little setback is a mark of strength, when a team can come back out and perform it shows great belief. We never rest on our laurels. We are a very, very tight team and we know exactly what we want to achieve. We believe in each other and we will go and get the job done.'

Australia's Kathryn Slattery forces Great Britain's Maddie Hinch into action at the 2016 Champions Trophy in London.
Frank Uijlenbroek

Chapter 5

Countdown to Rio

Following the completion of the Champions Trophy on 26 June, the Great Britain women's hockey team returned from London to their Bisham Abbey headquarters to finalise preparations for Rio 2016.

To many who had witnessed their disappointing performances at the Lee Valley Hockey & Tennis Centre in the Queen Elizabeth Olympic Park, Team GB's chances of winning an Olympic gold medal in Brazil appeared slim. With the hockey competition in Rio starting on 9 August 2016, the squad had a six-week window to right the wrongs of the Champions Trophy if they were to get anywhere near a podium finish. Time was definitely not on their side.

Despite a general feeling of frustration within the squad regarding their displays in London, the conviction in their potential to land the greatest prize in sport remained, according to midfield star Georgie Twigg, very much alive.

'Of course we wanted to win the Champions Trophy but we were also very realistic,' says Twigg. 'It was a stepping stone towards Rio and not performing in London gave us lots to reflect on. Things had to be said and done in a very short time frame, which meant that you simply couldn't hide from anything. Things needed to get better quickly, so in hindsight I really don't think it was a bad thing that we didn't do so well.

'Unsey (Laura Unsworth), Alex (Danson) and Lily (Owsley) were all recovering from injuries and it was their first tournament back in action,' Twigg continues. 'I think the tournament came at a very good time because it gave us the chance to play together, although clearly we were a little bit rusty and things did not exactly go to plan. We'd also had Olympic selection internally just before the Champions Trophy, and that would certainly have been a factor.'

Twigg's reference to the effect of Olympic selection was echoed by the words of assistant coach Craig Keegan, who says that the massive emotional and psychological impact on everyone connected to the squad could not be underestimated.

'We were one of the only teams that had already selected our squad and we knew that would play a part psychologically with the players,' says the Aussie goalscoring coach. 'There is emotional baggage that comes with selection, but once it is done there is a huge release of tension and enthusiasm. We talked about it both before and during the tournament, we knew there would be some issues around our ability to play at the top level because our selection process had already been done. You never know if the results would have been different if we had held back. I suspect that if you are playing for your Olympic place, then your mental state would be different.'

As he had done with his Olympic squad selections for both Beijing 2008 and London 2012, head coach Danny Kerry's decision-making process for Rio 2016 was made with painstaking thought and deliberation, making good use of Keegan and fellow assistant coach Karen Brown as sounding boards in the lengthy discussions about who would, and who would not, be on the plane to Brazil.

The team that Kerry believed could win Olympic gold was revealed to the world just two days after the completion of the Champions Trophy. Sixteen of the 18 athletes who represented Great Britain at that competition were named, with the remaining players being two of the three nominated non-playing reserve athletes.

In terms of experience, Kerry's selection was pure symmetry. Eight bronze medallists from London 2012 were joined by eight players who had made big impressions over the past four years. Team captain and central defender Kate Richardson-Walsh and midfielder Helen Richardson-Walsh would be competing in their fourth Olympic Games, with striker Alex Danson and defender Crista Cullen – one year after her surprise return to the training squad – being named to compete in a third Games. Fellow 2012 bronze medallists Hannah Macleod (forward), Georgie Twigg (midfielder), Laura Unsworth (defender) and Nicola White (forward) had also made the cut, with Olympic debutants Maddie Hinch (goalkeeper), Giselle Ansley (defender), Sophie Bray (forward), Shona McCallin

Kate Richardson-Walsh was selected for her fourth Olympic Games, following appearances at Sydney, Beijing and London.
Frank Uijlenbroek

Georgie Twigg expresses her frustration at the 2016 Champions Trophy.
Frank Uijlenbroek

Helen Richardson-Walsh defied all the odds to overcome a career beset by injuries and to be selected for Rio 2016.
Frank Uijlenbroek

(midfielder), Lily Owsley (forward), Sam Quek (defender), Susannah Townsend (midfielder) and Hollie Webb (defender) completing the line-up. Joie Leigh and Ellie Watton were named as the outfield non-playing reserves, being joined on the plane to Rio by goalkeeper Kirsty Mackay.

For the athletes selected for Rio it was a mixed bag of emotions. There was both relief and joy at knowing that they would be fulfilling a lifelong dream, but sadness in the knowledge that almost half of the 31-strong central squad would be feeling devastated at learning that, after years of gruelling training and sacrifice, they would not be going. London 2012 bronze medallists Ashleigh Ball and Emily Maguire were just two

of the players to miss out, with Scotland international Maguire expressing her own sadness in an interview with *The Sunday Herald* newspaper.

'We knew exactly when to expect the email, so you're just sitting waiting for that moment,' she told reporter Susan Egelstaff. 'I was in my flat with my boyfriend. He'd taken the afternoon off work so he could be there with me, which was really nice. You're just hanging on waiting for the email to come. It's horrible. I was gutted.

'I knew that I was on the fringes of the team. I wasn't really confident I was going to be picked because no-one's ever really sure of that. I was thinking I might be a reserve, that's what I had prepared myself

Goalkeeper Maddie Hinch and Hannah Macleod made the cut for Rio 2016.
Frank Uijlenbroek

for. So when I found out I wasn't even that I was like: "OK, it's worse than I'd thought."

'Having been to London and won a medal has definitely not made this any easier. Obviously I'm hugely proud of everything I've done and I know that I'm so fortunate to have had all the experiences that I've had. So yes, in the future, I'll look back on that and be proud but right now, it's very difficult to have that broad view.'

Another player to miss out on selection was Surbiton Hockey Club midfielder Sarah Haycroft, who found comfort in the knowledge that she, unlike Maguire who would announce her international retirement before the year was out, wanted to remain part of the cycle leading into the Tokyo 2020 Olympic Games.

'Having that ambition definitely helped me, although for those who were likely to retire after Rio it was harder,' says Haycroft. 'Yes, I was completely devastated that I wasn't part of the team that went out there, but I think all of us who didn't go knew that we had given so much to help get the team to the level that they were at.'

Forward Ellie Watton described her selection as one of the three non-playing reserve athletes as 'bittersweet'. Speaking to *The Derby Telegraph*, local paper to her first club Matlock HC, Watton said: 'Of course I'm pleased that I will be going to the Olympic Games and would love the chance to play, but that will only be if someone gets injured – and I don't want that

Giselle Ansley, seen in action here against Emily Wold of the USA, was selected for the Team GB side for Rio 2016.
Frank Uijlenbroek

to happen. We're a close bunch of girls. We always look out for each other and I think that shows on the pitch.'

For the players who were selected there now came an awareness of extra responsibility. Rio-bound defender Giselle Ansley says that the extraordinary attitude and approach of those athletes who did not gain selection left her feeling duty-bound to do everything in her power to not let them down.

'The girls who were not selected were incredible. They put their heart and soul into every training session, which really summed up the strength and unity of our group. It was a tough, tough situation for them but they pushed us so hard and continued to sacrifice everything for the cause. We all believed that the 16-player squad as well as the three reserves that went to Rio were representing the entire squad of 31, and we felt a huge sense of responsibility towards them because they had got us to where we were.'

Regarding her own selection, Ansley admits to feeling a sense of relief. To the watching commentators, the return of Crista Cullen to the central programme appeared to spell bad news for a defender with remarkably similar playing qualities.

'Before she came into the programme I'd never played with Crista, or even spoken to her, although I'd watched her from the stands at London 2012. I was worried that this person was coming into the group who was a penalty corner flicker and a defender, which was pretty much what I do. When she came in I could see that she had this great confidence and a presence. I remember admiring her a lot when she took me to one side and spoke to me about my concerns. We sat down and she said "I know what you are thinking, but I'm not here because I am certain to go. I have no idea if I'll go or not." I learned so much from her, she helped me with my flicking and with my mindset because she had done it so many times before.'

While Cullen was undoubtedly a player who had been there and done it, her inclusion in the Rio squad following a lack of pitch time at the Champions Trophy, where she suffered a competition-ending injury, left many scratching their heads. Cullen herself was in no doubt.

Emily Maguire (below) and Sarah Haycroft (above)
were unlucky to miss the cut for selection.
Frank Uijlenbroek

'I had torn some ligaments in my ankle and was wearing a protective boot, so yes, my pitch-time was limited because I was conscious of my situation knowing that I had to turn it around quickly to get fit,' says Cullen, whose five goals at London 2012 had seen her finish alongside Alex Danson as Team GB's top scorer. 'Ironically, I did exactly the same thing just before London 2012, but it was the other ankle. It wasn't ideal, but it was manageable and I was able to make sure that I could play a part in the Rio Olympics by getting it turned around in the time that I had. I think a lot of the media love to doubt people at different stages through their career and that is fine. Everyone is allowed to have their own opinion. I knew that I was in some of the best shape I've ever been in and I was unfortunate enough to have taken a knock, and that is life in sport. I'm pretty level headed and balanced. I knew I had been

through it before and I knew I had to get myself fit again and it wouldn't be an issue.'

Aside from the inclusion of Cullen, Kerry's 16-player squad consisted entirely of players who had stormed to the European title with England in 2015. Whilst clearly capable of winning on the big stage, a squad consisting entirely of English players – a situation mirrored by the men's selection – was certainly problematic for GB Hockey's chief operating officer Sally Munday.

'As soon as I became aware that both squads were going to be all English, I personally thought to myself that, from a GB perspective, this isn't great,' says Munday, who revealed that Scottish Hockey chief executive David Sweetman was distraught when she phoned to deliver the news. 'I really felt for him and it was a horrible call to make, as he was genuinely really, really upset.

'I really wished it was different, I genuinely did. I'd love to see us better represented, but I also know that, frankly, the coaches do not think about it like that, they genuinely don't. I don't mean that they don't care about it, they simply don't think politically. They pick the 16 players that they think are going to get a medal at the Olympic Games, and they think about that incredibly carefully. I'd much rather we had two squads of one nation than having a player there that had been selected purely to satisfy a political need.'

It was a situation that triggered Scottish Hockey to issue a media statement in a show of support and tribute to their affected athletes, recognising both the huge sacrifices that they had made and their contribution to the Team GB programme. Despite an understandably downhearted tone, the statement reflected Scottish Hockey's support of the Team GB squad that would compete in Rio as well as providing optimism about future Scottish athletes playing a central role in the next Olympic cycle. There was also an important point made about the officials who would be representing Scottish Hockey in Rio, with umpires Sarah Wilson and Martin Madden both being appointed for the Games alongside video umpire Andy Mair. Wilson and Madden would both go on to perform exceptionally in Brazil, deservingly earning the honour of officiating the bronze medal matches.

'People have said to me that the proof is in the pudding and the women won gold, but I would counter that and say that the men came ninth, so you could argue that we should have picked a different men's squad,' says Munday on reflection. 'Equally, the coaches could have picked three or four different players and had the same outcome. I trust and believe in the process, which is important.'

While Danny Kerry had made a squad selection based purely on the athletes he believed were the right ones for the job in hand, he admits that leaving out Scotland's Emily Maguire was one of the toughest choices he had faced. 'It was a hugely difficult decision not to select Emily because she was an athlete with Olympic experience, a very good defender and a member of the leadership group. Her trajectory was up and down and if the Olympic Games had happened a month later, she may well have gone. The political ramifications of selecting all-English players did not come into it, it was about selecting the best players at the time.'

Unsurprisingly for a man renowned for obsessing over every detail in order for his teams to achieve the best possible outcome, Kerry put everything that he had learned from his two previous Olympic campaigns at Beijing 2008 and London 2012 into his planned

Joie Leigh was named as a Team GB reserve athlete for Rio 2016.
Frank Uijlenbroek

assault on the gold medal in Brazil. Every scenario had been vigorously assessed and analysed, so much so that one of the first things that the athletes would do upon their arrival in Rio de Janeiro would be to work out how many footsteps it would take to get from their accommodation to the dining hall in an attempt to keep energy expenditure to an absolute minimum. For the record, that journey was just over 1,000 steps each way. Another example would be the re-laying of the training pitch at Bisham Abbey, with the new surface perfectly matching the blue with green trim they would

encounter at Rio's Deodoro Olympic Hockey Centre.

'The pitch at Bisham was knackered and so It made sense to have the Rio pitch,' says Kerry looking back at the decision. 'The irony for me was that we had to be careful not to over-prepare the athletes. The danger is that the athletes don't develop the resilience necessary to succeed. When everything is on tap it is easy and the Olympic environment is sub-optimal a lot of the time.'

With both the women's and men's hockey squads opting not to join the Team GB holding camp in Belo Horizonte on the grounds that there was no pitch and no opposition to play against – another call made by Kerry in a bid to ensure the best possible preparation – the Rio imitation surface at Bisham Abbey was put to good use. One final fitness session saw the entire squad working out in Rio-themed fancy dress, with Maddie Hinch broadcasting the colourful show, albeit briefly, live on Facebook. The footage provided wonderful insight into the mood of the camp, which was clearly buoyant. The team were as ready as they would ever be, and the time to deliver on their potential had arrived.

The Great Britain women's hockey squad for Rio 2016

Goalkeepers

1 **Maddie Hinch** Holcombe HC
Home town: West Chiltington, West Sussex

2 **Kirsty Mackay** East Grinstead HC
(Non-playing reserve)
Home town: Blackpool, Lancashire

Defenders

4 **Laura Unsworth** East Grinstead HC
Home town: Sutton Coldfield, West Midlands

5 **Crista Cullen** No Club
Home town: London/Kenya

11 **Kate Richardon-Walsh** Reading HC
Home town: Stockport, Manchester

13 **Sam Quek** Holcombe HC
Home town: Wirral, Merseyside

18 **Giselle Ansley** Surbiton HC
Home town: Kingsbridge, Devon

20 **Hollie Webb** Surbiton HC
Home town: Belper, Derbyshire

Midfielders

7 **Georgie Twigg** Surbiton HC
Home town: Lincoln, Lincolnshire

8 **Helen Richardson-Walsh** Reading HC
Home town: West Bridgford, Nottinghamshire

9 **Susannah Townsend** Canterbury HC
Home town: Egerton, Kent

14 **Joie Leigh** Clifton Robinsons HC
(Non-playing reserve)
Home town: Huddersfield, West Yorkshire

24 **Shona McCallin** Holcombe HC
Home town: Newark, Nottinghamshire

Forwards

6 **Hannah Macleod** St Albans HC
Home town: Maidenhead, Berkshire

15 **Alex Danson** Reading HC
Home town: Odiham, Hampshire

19 **Sophie Bray** East Grinstead HC
Home town: Claygate, Surrey

21 **Ellie Watton** Holcombe HC
(Non-playing reserve)
Home town: Maidenhead, Berkshire

26 **Lily Owsley** University of Birmingham HC
Home town: Bristol

28 **Nicola White** Holcombe HC
Home town: Oldham, Greater Manchester

Chapter 6

The Games Begin

To win bronze in London was great, but we want to not go one better, but two better. We'd love to come home with that gold medal, but every squad heading out there will have exactly the same thoughts as us. I am very proud to be representing Great Britain and even though it's my fourth time appearing at a Games, the pride that it fills you with never wears off.

Helen Richardson-Walsh ahead of the Rio 2016 Olympic Games

Team GB women's hockey team jetted out to Rio de Janeiro on Wednesday 27 July, 11 days before the start of the Olympic title challenge. A chance meeting with Jamaican sprint king Usain Bolt at London Heathrow Airport was the perfect start to the trip, with a star-struck Maddie Hinch describing the entire situation as 'totally surreal'.

Following a productive settling in period coupled with positive training match performances against China and Spain, it was soon down to the daily business of meticulous planning, preparation and calculated decision-making that would give Team GB the very best chance of Olympic success. It was an approach that would ultimately prove successful, but came with a degree of sacrifice.

Team GB's first match of the competition would take place on Saturday 6 August, less than 24 hours after the Opening Ceremony of the Rio 2016 Olympic Games. Attendance at the Opening Ceremony is a proud moment in the career of most Olympians, but the proximity to matchday one ultimately led to the group decision that it was simply too much of a risk to take.

'As soon as the match schedule came out we knew it was never going to happen,' wrote Hinch in her blog on the BBC website ahead of the Opening Ceremony. 'It's my first Olympic Games so I was gutted, but we listened to the girls who've been before and they told us the effect it can have on you, standing up for four hours when you are playing the next day. We've made the right call.'

The athletes and staff ahead of their flight to Rio de Janeiro.
Team GB Hockey

Kate Richardson-Walsh leads out her team for the opening match of their Olympic title challenge against Australia.
Frank Uijlenbroek

Saturday 6 August 2016
Team GB v Australia
Match 1 (pool phase)

With preparations complete and unnecessary exertions avoided, the long wait for the competition to begin was almost over. Now it was time to perform and, with 2014 World Cup silver medallists Australia being their first opponents, they needed to deliver. With six teams competing for four quarter-final places in each pool, failure to get points on the board early could prove catastrophic.

Six weeks had passed since the two nations had squared up in London at the Champions Trophy. That had been a match dominated virtually start to finish by the Hockeyroos, who recorded a comprehensive 4-1 victory to condemn the hosts to a morale-crushing fourth defeat on the bounce. This time around they would face each other on the greatest stage of all, one where the Australians had taken the gold medal on three occasions. Their silver medal at the Rabobank Hockey World Cup 2014 in The Hague, Netherlands, had provided plenty of evidence that the Olympic champions of 1988, 1996 and 2000 were once again a team to be feared.

Head coach Adam Commens – himself a former Australia men's international with the Kookaburras – was targeting the top of the podium in what he had already confirmed would be his final competition in charge of the side. At number three in the world rankings, four places above a GB side that had fallen to seventh following their disappointing Champions Trophy campaign, it came as little surprise that the champions of Oceania were not just favourites to beat the Brits, they were genuine contenders for gold.

Despite their dominant display against Great Britain in London, Australia's Champions Trophy campaign had ended in disappointment. Their shootout defeat at the hands of the USA in a bronze medal match was made even more painful by the fact that they had managed to squander a 2-0 lead in the contest. For Great Britain, their victory over New Zealand in the 5-6 classification game had restored belief and re-energised the group. Although the personnel had

A trademark attacking run from Sophie Bray causes problems for Australia.

Frank Uijlenbroek

Team GB rush to congratulate goalscorer Lily Owsley.
Frank Uijlenbroek

not changed, it soon became clear that in Rio, Australia faced a Team GB side with a very different mindset to the one they encountered in London.

The match itself, played under the evening floodlights at the Deodoro Hockey Centre, was tense, twitchy and utterly absorbing. The Australians started at breakneck speed and had the better of the opening two quarters but found themselves up against a British defensive unit – expertly marshalled by captain Kate Richardson-Walsh – at the top of their game. Goalkeeper Maddie Hinch gave an early indication of the pivotal role that she would play in Team GB's Olympic campaign with three crucial saves, while the ever-fearless Crista Cullen soon silenced those who questioned her inclusion with a typical show of bravery, charging down a fierce strike from prolific goalscorer Jodie Kenny to stop the Hockeyroos from making the first mark on the scoresheet.

Midfield stalwart Helen Richardson-Walsh also played her part in keeping the Australian onslaught at bay, making a vital goal-line save before the Brits landed a sucker-punch four minutes before half-time.

A slick passing move involving Hollie Webb, Shona McCallin and Sophie Bray ripped through the heart of the Australian defence before Lily Owsley showed composure beyond her years to produce a cool finish and give Team GB a shock lead. It was a special moment for Owsley, the FIH Rising Star of the Year for 2015, who after the game remarked that as far as Saturday nights go as a 21-year-old, scoring on her Olympic debut would take some beating.

Team GB's 1-0 advantage was almost cancelled out seconds later by Australia defender and penalty corner expert Georgina Morgan, who rattled the frame of the British goal just ahead of half-time. It proved to be a sign of things to come, with Morgan finally finding a way past Hinch early in the third quarter with an unstoppable flick into the top corner.

Although the equaliser was no more than Australia deserved, Team GB were undeterred and regained the advantage towards the end of the third quarter. A matter of minutes after Australia were reduced to ten players due to a yellow card suspension to defender Edwina Bone, a flowing counter-attack

Team GB rush to congratulate goalscorer Lily Owsley.
Frank Uijlenbroek

carved open the Hockeyroos back-line to release striker Alex Danson, who turned onto her favoured backhand and rifled the ball home with power and precision to make the score 2-1. Despite a nervy final quarter, which saw Maddie Hinch again called into action, Danson's killer instinct in front of goal had yet again proved decisive as Team GB kicked off their gold medal challenge in style with a first-ever win over Australia in women's hockey at the Olympic Games.

'It was a good three points for us,' said Kate Richardson-Walsh, speaking to BBC Sport after the match. 'It was a difficult game and it was not pretty at times, but we stayed disciplined throughout. Australia are a fantastic side. They have strength all over the field and they will do very well in this tournament, so to get a win against them is definitely a great confidence booster.'

Australian media coverage reported that the Hockeyroos were desperately unlucky in their 'shock defeat' to Team GB, a side that had ridden their luck in the contest. In many respects, they were right. The statistics backed up the argument that the Aussies had dominated in terms of possession, penalty corners and shots on goal, the latter being as much as 20 - 4 in Australia's favour. The counter-argument is that the only statistic that truly matters is the final score, and Team GB's extraordinary work-rate combined with an ability to make the most of their goalscoring opportunities proved to be conclusive. It was a triumph earned through grit, determination and discipline, traits that would become a constant feature throughout their campaign in Rio. The result reaffirmed the team's belief that even in the most pressurised situations and when their backs are placed firmly up against the wall, they knew that they were capable of battling through and emerging victorious.

Pool B Result

Team GB	**2-1**	**Australia**
Lily Owsley 26m FG		Georgina Morgan 33m PC
Alex Danson 43m FG		

Pool results and standings from first round of matches

Pool A
7 August: New Zealand 4-1 Korea
7 August: Netherlands 5-0 Spain
7 August: China 1-1 Germany

Pos.	Team	Pld	W	D	L	GF	GA	GD	Pts
1	Netherlands	1	1	0	0	5	0	+5	3
2	New Zealand	1	1	0	0	4	1	+3	3
3	China	1	0	1	0	1	1	0	1
4	Germany	1	0	1	0	1	1	0	1
5	Korea	1	0	0	1	1	4	-3	0
6	Spain	1	0	0	1	0	5	-5	0

Pool B
6 August: Argentina 1-2 USA
6 August: Team GB 2-1 Australia
7 August: Japan 2-2 India

Pos.	Team	Pld	W	D	L	GF	GA	GD	Pts
1	Team GB	1	1	0	0	2	1	+1	3
2	USA	1	1	0	0	2	1	+1	3
3	India	1	0	1	0	2	2	0	1
4	Japan	1	0	1	0	2	2	0	1
5	Argentina	1	0	0	1	1	2	-1	0
6	Australia	1	0	0	1	1	2	-1	0

Giselle Ansley slams home a penalty corner effort against India.
Frank Uijlenbroek

Monday 8 August 2016
India v Team GB
Match 2 (pool phase)

Such is the relentless nature of the hockey competitions at the Olympic Games, it was not long before the team were back in action. Just two days after their victory against the third-ranked Australians, Team GB faced a completely different challenge in India, at 13th, the lowest ranked nation in the women's competition. It was a match that Danny Kerry's side were widely expected to win, but any level of complacency had the potential to prove costly. India – known as the 'Eves' – had started their Olympic campaign with a respectable and fully deserved point against tenth ranked Japan, with star striker Rani getting among the goals as her side overturned a 2-0 deficit to claim a 2-2 draw against the 'Cherry Blossoms'. Under the guidance of former Australian head coach

Neil Hawgood, India were playing their best hockey in years and in 21-year-old Rani, who had already competed in more than 150 senior internationals and registered more than 80 goals, they had one of the most feared strikers in the game. If Team GB played to their potential, they would surely prove too strong for India. If they did not, India were capable of inflicting some serious damage to their gold medal challenge and dissipating the confidence drawn from the win over Australia, a fact known only too well by Helen and Kate Richardson-Walsh.

Fourteen years earlier, in the summer of 2002, youngsters Helen Richardson and Kate Walsh were both part of a monumental achievement as England recorded a stunning 2-1 victory over the

Alex Danson assesses her options as she drives forward. ▶
Frank Uijlenbroek

Team-mates celebrate with Ansley.
Frank Uijlenbroek

then Olympic champions Australia in the semi-finals of the Commonwealth Games in Manchester. Following that success and playing on home soil, it was almost seen as a formality that England would prove themselves to be too strong for surprise finalists India. Remarkably, it was the Indians who took home the gold medal thanks to a golden goal in extra time from Mamta Kharab. It was an epic victory that was so much against the odds it even inspired the hit Indian sports movie *Chak De! India* (English: Go for it! India), about a coach who turns a talented but disorganised Indian women's national hockey team into a championship-winning unit. Could history repeat itself?

Any fears that the team might take India too lightly at Rio 2016 proved to be completely unfounded. Team GB were totally dominant, forcing India deep into their own territory for long periods before eventually opening the scoring thanks to defender Giselle Ansley, who scored her first Olympic goal with a penalty corner flick in the 25th minute. A second goal arrived just two minutes later, with Nicola

White forcing home from close range after excellent attacking work from Alex Danson and Sophie Bray. Shortly after half-time, Danson made the score 3-0 with her 95th international goal after being supplied by Lily Owsley, who showed quick hands to carve open the Indian back-line before supplying the perfect pass for her team-mate to effectively end the contest.

'There's no way we would ever be complacent, the players and staff wouldn't stand for it,' said team captain Kate Richardson-Walsh after a victory which moved her side level with the USA at the top of Pool B with a maximum six points from two matches. 'We are here to represent Great Britain, and all 31 of us in the central programme go out there with pride every time we play or train. We're taking one game at a time. We've spent many hours talking about our culture, our behaviours and having a gold medal mentality, we live for that and it shows on the field.'

Crista Cullen puts her body on the line to deny India's Lilima.
Frank Uijlenbroek

Pool B Result

India	0-3	**Team GB**

Giselle Ansley 25m PC
Nicola White 27m FG
Alex Danson 33m FG

Pool results and standings from second round of matches

Pool A
8 August 2016: New Zealand 1-2 Germany
8 August 2016: Netherlands 4-0 Korea
8 August 2016: Spain 0-2 China

Pos.	Team	Pld	W	D	L	GF	GA	GD	Pts
1	Netherlands	2	2	0	0	9	0	+9	6
2	China	2	1	1	0	3	1	+2	4
3	Germany	2	1	1	0	3	2	+1	4
4	New Zealand	2	1	0	1	5	3	+2	3
5	Korea	2	0	0	2	1	8	-7	0
6	Spain	2	0	0	2	0	7	-7	0

Pool B
8 August 2016: Australia 1-2 USA
8 August 2016: India 0-3 Team GB
8 August 2016: Argentina 4-0 Japan

Pos.	Team	Pld	W	D	L	GF	GA	GD	Pts
1	Team GB	2	2	0	0	5	1	+4	6
2	USA	2	2	0	0	4	2	+2	6
3	Argentina	2	1	0	1	5	2	+3	3
4	India	2	0	1	1	2	5	-3	1
5	Japan	2	0	1	1	2	6	-4	1
6	Australia	2	0	0	2	2	4	-2	0

Milestone moment for Hollie Webb, who is recognised for her 100th international appearance ahead of Team GB's crucial pool clash with Argentina.
Koen Suyk

Wednesday 10 August 2016
Team GB v Argentina
Match 3 (pool phase)

While the 'gold medal mentality' referred to by Kate Richardson-Walsh had been clearly evident in Team GB's opening two matches, it would definitely need to come to the fore in match three.

At number two in the world, Argentina were the top ranked team in Pool B and, thanks to their superb success at the Champions Trophy in London, arrived

in Rio de Janeiro sensing that this could be their year. With six of the last seven Champions Trophy titles going Argentina's way, not to mention a silver medal at the London 2012 Olympics, bronze at the Rabobank Hockey World Cup 2014 and winning the 2015 Hockey World League, their hopes of landing a first Olympic title were not unwarranted. It came as little surprise that

Despite Argentina's excellent pre-Olympic form, Team GB had plenty of reasons to believe that they could overcome the giants of South American hockey. The meeting between the two sides at the Champions Trophy just six weeks earlier had ended with the score locked at 2-2, while in 2015 Great Britain had defeated the Argentines on their way to winning the Hockey World League Semi-Final event in Valencia, Spain to book their ticket to Rio.

Despite a huge fan presence in Rio thanks to the relative proximity of Argentina to Brazil, Las Leonas did not make the best of starts to their own Olympic campaign, falling to a 2-1 loss against a USA side that had also beaten them to gold at the 2015 Pan American Games in Toronto, Canada. However, the side bounced back with a sparkling 4-0 victory over Japan, with penalty corner expert Noel Barrionuevo scoring twice alongside open play efforts from rising star Maria Granatto and Rebecchi.

The outcome of the meeting between Team GB and Argentina was likely to have serious repercussions on their respective destinies at Rio 2016. A win would significantly enhance the possibilities of an all-important top two finish in Pool B, which would result in avoiding the top two teams in Pool A in the quarter-final cross-overs. Suffer defeat, and the already difficult journey to the gold medal game would become even more arduous.

As per their meeting with Australia, Team GB were in for another night of high drama. In an evenly contested first quarter, Argentina went closest to opening the scoring when Delfina Merino moved past Maddie Hinch before hitting the frame of the British goal. It was a glorious opportunity wasted and would cost Argentina dearly, with Team GB producing a dominant second quarter performance to open up a 2-0 lead thanks to two goals in three minutes from veteran midfielder Helen Richardson-Walsh.

Her first was a well-taken penalty corner deflection before her close-range second put the Brits firmly in control at the break. Crucial saves from Hinch either side of half-time ensured that Team GB's two-goal cushion remained intact, an advantage that was extended even further when Sophie Bray made it 3-0 early in the third quarter.

If a three-goal advantage was good enough to kill Team GB's contest against India two days earlier, any hopes of it doing the same against the brilliant Argentinians were soon ended when 2014 FIH Young Women's Player of the Year Florencia Habif scored twice in two minutes to bring her side back into contention going into what would prove to be an intense, breathless fourth and final quarter. Yellow card suspensions handed out to Susannah Townsend and Sophie Bray saw Team

the retirement of legendary attacker and eight-time World Player of the Year Luciana Aymar shortly after the 2014 Hockey World Cup would lead to a period of readjustment for 'Las Leonas' (The Lionesses), but by early 2016 there was no doubt that the team, coached by former Argentina men's international Gabriel Minadeo, had rediscovered their best form. A 2-1 victory over Olympic and world champions the Netherlands in the final of the Champions Trophy was noteworthy, while extraordinary attacker and team captain Carla Rebecchi had been almost unstoppable as she claimed the best player and top scorer prizes at that event.

Sam Quek shows full commitment to deny Argentina captain Carla Rebecchi.
Frank Uijlenbroek

GB reduced to nine players, and it seemed only a matter of time before Argentina would get the equaliser. Remarkably, the brilliant British defence weathered the storm and had a glorious chance to add a fourth when a breakaway opportunity resulted in a penalty stroke. Helen Richardson-Walsh stepped up to the mark, but was denied her hat-trick thanks to a fine block from Argentina goalkeeper Belen Succi. Team GB found themselves defending desperately in the final stages, but held on to secure another excellent win that would serve to boost their confidence even further.

'We're really pleased to get the three points,' said Helen Richardson-Walsh after the contest. 'Argentina are a really good team so we expected them to come back. We tried not to concede the goals but it is what it is. We're really pleased to get the job done in the end.

'I'm annoyed about the stroke but pleased to get the goals I did get,' continued the midfielder, before making a prophetic comment. 'Fortunately it didn't cost us but hopefully I'll save that goal for another game.'

Georgie Twigg stays low.
Frank Uijlenbroek

Time stands still as Sophie Bray shoots for goal.
Koen Suyk

This third successive victory at Rio 2016, which arrived exactly four years to the day after their brilliant bronze medal at London 2012, was enough to guarantee a place in the quarter-finals. It also ensured that the team kept pace with high-flying USA at the top of Pool B, with both sides having claimed a maximum nine points.

To those on the outside looking in, the showdown with the Americans in Team GB's fifth and final match of the pool phase was grabbing everyone's attention, and with good reason. It would almost certainly decide the winner of Pool B, which came with the prize of a quarter-final meeting against the fourth-placed finisher in Pool A. However, as with the India match, Team GB's coaching staff had no intention of even for one moment allowing anyone within the camp to be distracted. Thoughts about USA were forbidden, and Team GB's opponents in their fourth match were certainly not to be underestimated.

Helen Richardson-Walsh scored twice as Team GB emerged triumphant over the pool's top-ranked team.
Koen Suyk

Fans of Team GB and Argentina watching the action unfold.
Koen Suyk

Pool B Result

Team GB	**3-2**	**Argentina**
Helen Richardson-Walsh		Florencia Habif
23m PC, 25m FG		41m FG, 42m FG
Sophie Bray 38m FG		

Pool results and standings from third round of matches

Pool A

10 August 2016: Spain 1-2 New Zealand
10 August 2016: Germany 2-0 Korea
10 August 2016: China 0-1 Netherlands

Pos.	Team	Pld	W	D	L	GF	GA	GD	Pts
1	Netherlands	3	3	0	0	10	0	+10	9
2	Germany	3	2	1	0	5	2	+3	7
3	New Zealand	3	2	0	1	7	4	+3	6
4	China	3	1	1	1	3	2	+1	4
5	Spain	3	0	0	3	1	9	-8	0
6	Korea	3	0	0	3	1	10	-9	0

Pool B

10 August 2016: India 1-6 Australia
10 August 2016: Team GB 3-2 Argentina
10 August 2016: USA 6-1 Japan

Pos.	Team	Pld	W	D	L	GF	GA	GD	Pts
1	USA	3	3	0	0	10	3	+7	9
2	Team GB	3	3	0	0	8	3	+5	9
3	Australia	3	1	0	2	8	5	+3	3
4	Argentina	3	1	0	2	7	5	+2	3
5	India	3	0	1	2	3	11	-8	1
6	Japan	3	0	1	2	3	12	-9	1

Lily Owsley's opening goal against Japan is enjoyed by Team GB.
Frank Uijlenbroek

Thursday 11 August 2016
Team GB v Japan
Match 4 (pool phase)

As had been the case ahead of their matches against Australia, India and Argentina, Team GB's preparations for their meeting with Japan were as meticulous as ever. Video analysis of the Japanese team had been completed, the game plan was hatched and every individual knew exactly what their role was in order to beat the tenth-ranked team in the world.

The Cherry Blossoms had not enjoyed a good start to their own Olympic challenge, managing to claim only one point from their opening three matches and having suffered a 6-1 thrashing against USA in their previous match. They were a team fighting for their Olympic survival, wholly aware that points against Team GB – a team that had crushed them 4-0 at London 2012 – were essential if they were to have any chance of booking their ticket to the quarter-finals.

Team GB needed just five minutes to take the lead in the contest, with the ever-lively Lily Owsley firing the ball across the face of the goal to force an error from experienced Japanese defender Miyuki Nakagawa, who could only divert into her own net. It was a lead that Team GB deserved, but one that they would not be able to extend until five minutes from full time thanks to a stunning overhead smash from Nicola White, with the Mancunian forward showing lightning-quick reactions to volley home, following a saved penalty corner effort from Crista Cullen.

White's special strike gave Team GB some much-needed breathing space just when it seemed that the second goal was never going to come. Despite their supremacy, the British struggled to find a way past Japanese shot-stopper Sakiyo Asano – who produced at least two saves that even Team GB custodian Maddie Hinch would have been proud of – and that was a concern. Hinch herself had been forced into action more times than she would have wanted, but ended the game

Crista Cullen and Hollie Webb show their joy as Nicola White scores against Japan.
Frank Uijlenbroek

Elation as Nicola White scores the all-important second
goal to seal victory against Japan. .
Frank Uijlenbroek

with her second clean sheet in four matches. Although the team had achieved a fourth straight victory and were now assured of a top two finish in Pool B, Danny Kerry was far from impressed by what he had witnessed.

'I don't think any of us would be satisfied with the performance; one or two players had to play well,' said an irritated Kerry immediately after the match, before going on to underline the important role played by his defensive line in the win. 'Laura Unsworth played well, played a mature game and Hollie Webb was also very solid, while Maddie also made some important saves, but I don't think anyone will be happy with the team performance.'

Shona McCallin on the charge against Japan.
Frank Uijlenbroek

Alex Danson in control.
Frank Uijlenbroek

Despite his obvious frustrations, Kerry accepted that being able to 'win ugly' was no bad thing. 'We've kept a clean sheet, won the game and not played that well. So, looking at the big picture, we've won four group games, we're definitely in the top two in the pool, so if you'd offered us that we'd have taken it every day. Today we had to create our own energy and tempo but we didn't do that. USA play a high tempo game, and I look forward to those kind of games.'

Japan struggled to stay with the pace of the Team GB side.
Frank Uijlenbroek

Pool B Result

Japan	0-2	Team GB
		Lily Owsley 5m FG
		Nicola White 55m PC

Pool results and standings from fourth round of matches

Pool A

11 August 2016: Germany 1-2 Spain
12 August 2016: Korea 0-0 China
12 August 2016: New Zealand 1-1 Netherlands

Pos.	Team	Pld	W	D	L	GF	GA	GD	Pts
1	Netherlands	4	3	0	1	11	1	+10	10
2	New Zealand	4	2	1	1	8	5	+3	7
3	Germany	4	2	1	1	6	4	+2	7
4	China	4	1	2	1	3	2	+1	5
5	Spain	4	1	0	3	3	10	-7	3
6	Korea	4	0	1	3	1	10	-9	1

Pool B

11 August 2016: Australia 1-0 Argentina
11 August 2016: USA 3-0 India
11 August 2016: Japan 0-2 Great Britain

Pos.	Team	Pld	W	D	L	GF	GA	GD	Pts
1	USA	4	4	0	0	13	3	+10	12
2	Great Britain	4	4	0	0	10	3	+7	12
3	Australia	4	2	0	2	9	5	+4	6
4	Argentina	4	1	0	3	7	6	+1	3
5	India	4	0	1	3	3	14	-11	1
6	Japan	4	0	1	3	3	14	-11	1

Saturday 13 August 2016

Team GB v USA
Match 5 (pool phase)

Although the victory against Japan was not entirely to Danny Kerry's liking, with four wins on the bounce, it was apparent that his team were gathering some serious momentum at Rio 2016. A guaranteed top two finish in Pool B was an achievement in itself, ensuring that they would avoid the two highest finishers in Pool A when it came to the cross-over quarter-finals.

Depending on the outcome of their final pool game, Team GB's quarter-final opponents would be either the third- or fourth-placed team in Pool A. To keep his squad's focus planted firmly 'in the now', Kerry says that he had requested that his players and staff did not look at the results or tables from the opposite pool. 'The

players learned their lesson in a tournament a few years back not to tune in to other teams,' he explains. Yet, with a minimum second place finish in Pool B now certain, Kerry allowed his staff and players to glance over at what had been happening in Pool A, and it made for interesting reading.

Going into the final day of pool action, the top three placings in Pool A were pretty much as predicted. Reigning Olympic and world champions the Netherlands were leading the charge ahead of world number four side New Zealand in second and 2004 Olympic and 2013 European champions Germany in third; positions which looked unlikely to change. However, the race for Pool A's fourth position was very much alive, with sixth-ranked China and 14th-ranked Spain both in contention. China, the Olympic silver medallists from Beijing 2008, were occupying that all-important fourth position, although

USA's Kelsey Kolojejchick under pressure from Team GB's Hollie Webb.
Frank Uijlenbroek

their place in the quarter-finals was under serious threat. Spain's 'Red Sticks', the Barcelona 1992 Olympic gold medallists, were just outside the quarter-final spots but in the perfect position to strike. A win in their final match against the already eliminated and utterly demoralised Korea would move the Spaniards ahead of China, leaving the Asian giants with the unenviable task of claiming at least a point against in-form New Zealand to secure their safe passage through to the last eight.

Team GB knew that they would face either Germany, China or Spain in the quarter-finals, but in truth that knowledge mattered little. Their victories over Australia and Argentina had proven that they were capable of challenging the very best in the world. The mantra would remain consistent. 'Take every game as it comes, keep on winning and the rest will look after itself.'

Like Team GB, the USA had plenty of momentum driving their Olympic title challenge forward. They had built on their superb bronze medal at the Champions

Trophy in London just six weeks earlier by recording four straight victories in Rio and, thanks to their superior goal difference, came into their Pool B decider against Team GB needing just a draw to confirm a first-place finish. With 13 goals scored and just three conceded, the USA were clearly on their game and in Katie Bam, who had scored five goals in her previous two matches, the Americans had a rare talent that needed to be closely monitored at all times.

While Bam was a major threat on the field, USA's biggest asset was undoubtedly present on the side-lines. Thanks to being a key member of the backroom staff that led Team GB to the Beijing 2008 and London 2012 Olympic Games as well as multiple podium finishes on the international stage between 2007 and 2012, USA head coach Craig Parnham possessed detailed knowledge of the inner workings of Team GB, from the players and tactics to their strengths and even their weaknesses. It was something that Danny Kerry was all

A delighted Hannah Macleod welcomes Sophie Bray and Alex Danson with open arms.
Frank Uijlenbroek

Lily Owsley puts her 3D skills to good use against the USA.
Frank Uijlenbroek

too aware of, so much so that it forced him into an unprecedented move when the two sides met earlier in the year at the Champions Trophy. Kerry deliberately refused to reveal his hand, sending his players out with a completely different game plan to what he had in mind for their Olympic meeting. Great Britain fell to a 2-0 loss, a painful result for Kerry's players but one that had ensured Parnham was none the wiser for their crucial grudge match in Brazil.

'It hurt some of the players hard in London, they understandably wanted to win in front of a home crowd, but I didn't want to reveal our tactics so I sent them out there to play a totally different game,' says Kerry, looking back on the defeat at the Champions Trophy. 'It wasn't a case of the team not trying to win, they were just trying to win differently. Yes, we might have lost in London, but we wiped them off the park in Rio.' Months down the line and it is hard for the Team GB coach to keep the smile from his face at the memory of that match.

Historically, meetings between Great Britain and the USA at earlier Olympic Games had been notoriously tight affairs, and the head-to-head in Rio continued along the same lines. The USA went close

A roar of delight from Alex Danson after scoring Team GB's second goal against the USA.
Frank Uijlenbroek

Five wins from five sealed a first-place finish in Pool B, much to the delight of the players and coaching staff.
Frank Uijlenbroek

early on with Bam firing fractionally wide of the target before midfielder Melissa Gonzalez was denied by the ever-alert Maddie Hinch. Crista Cullen, who was making her 100th appearance in British colours, forced two penalty corner saves from American shot-stopper Jackie Briggs towards the end of a frenetic and physical opening quarter.

Team GB controlled the second and third periods but could not find a way past the inspired Briggs, who denied Sophie Bray, Alex Danson and Nicola White with crucial saves before the deadlock was finally broken, although not by the Brits. With six minutes of the third quarter remaining, USA striker Michelle Vittese pounced on a loose ball and found the bottom right corner with a strike of unerring accuracy to put the Americans firmly in the driving seat going into the final quarter.

For all of Team GB's endeavour (and tactical secrecy in London), it was beginning to look increasingly likely that Craig Parnham was once again going to put one over his former employers. In the final quarter, time seemed to be ticking by at triple speed, and Team GB soon found themselves needing two goals in the last ten minutes to change their destiny and avoid a likely face-off against Germany in the quarter-finals.

With nine minutes remaining, USA goalscorer Michelle Vittese was given a yellow card five-minute suspension and, with an extra player on the field, Team GB exploited the opportunity with devastating effect. Two goals arrived in quick succession, with Sophie Bray converting a slick penalty corner routine in the 53rd minute before Alex Danson made the most of a terrific pass from Sam Quek to move her team into a 2-1 lead with four minutes left to play.

A first-place finish in the pool was now theirs to lose, but the drama was not over yet. Moments after Danson's strike, the match swung dramatically back in the favour of the USA when Georgie Twigg was shown a yellow card before Hinch made a crucial late save from USA captain Lauren Crandall. In the final minute, Susannah Townsend joined Twigg in the sin bin as Team GB finished with nine players, but even that was not enough to deny Kerry's team yet another victory to finish at the Pool B summit with a maximum 15 points in the bag. The team had achieved what had seemed almost unimaginable just six weeks earlier. A fantastic five wins out of five was a dream scenario, one that gave them the best possible chance of getting themselves among the medals in Rio.

'If you'd offered us top spot in the pool at the start of the week I'd have bitten your hand off,' said captain Kate Richardson-Walsh immediately after the

Goalscorers Sophie Bray and Alex Danson enjoy the moment.
Frank Uijlenbroek

triumph. 'The momentum we've created is good. All the sides are excellent in this tournament so I'm really proud of what we've done so far. In all of the games we've shown a bit of difference in what we can do. We've been goals up, goals down, played with ten and played with nine. We're showing we can do all kinds of hockey; now we want to play at our best. In order to succeed, we need to listen to the tactics. Danny Kerry is a fantastic tactician. If we do what he asks of us, we'll be fine.'

The unsatisfactory performances of the Champions Trophy were all but a distant memory, and the momentum Susannah Townsend had hoped to pick up in London had finally arrived. In truth, the timing was perfect. The group that had never stopped trusting in their capabilities were on a roll, and the players knew that from here on in anything was possible.

Pool B Result

Team GB	**2-1**	**USA**
Sophie Bray 53m PC		Michelle Vittese 39m FG
Alex Danson 56m FG		

Pool results and standings from fifth round of matches

Pool A

13 August 2016: Netherlands 2-0 Germany
13 August 2016: Korea 2-3 Spain
13 August 2016: China 0-3 New Zealand

Pos.	Team	Pld	W	D	L	GF	GA	GD	Pts
1	Netherlands	5	4	1	0	13	1	+12	13
2	New Zealand	5	3	1	1	11	5	+6	10
3	Germany	5	2	1	2	6	6	0	7
4	Spain	5	2	0	3	6	12	–6	6
5	China	5	1	2	2	3	5	–2	5
6	South Korea	5	0	1	4	3	13	–10	1

Pool B

13 August 2016: Argentina 5-0 India
13 August 2016: Team GB 2-1 USA
13 August 2016: Australia 2-0 Japan

Pos.	Team	Pld	W	D	L	GF	GA	GD	Pts
1	Team GB	5	5	0	0	12	4	+8	15
2	USA	5	4	0	1	14	5	+9	12
3	Australia	5	3	0	2	11	5	+6	9
4	Argentina	5	2	0	3	12	6	+6	6
5	Japan	5	0	1	4	3	16	–13	1
6	India	5	0	1	4	3	19	-16	1

Chapter 7

The Quarter-Finals

I n the hours that immediately followed their table-topping Pool B triumph over the Americans, Danny Kerry and his squad waited patiently to learn who they would face in the quarter-finals of the Rio 2016 Olympic Games.

Team GB's challengers would be the team that finished fourth in Pool A, a position occupied by Spain – the 1992 Olympic champions but the lowest-ranked team in the competition at 14th in the world – following their 3-2 win over bottom-of-the-table Korea earlier in the day. That result was bad news for China, forcing the world's sixth-best team outside of the quarter-final qualification spots just hours before their showdown with New Zealand, a team that came into the match in high spirits thanks to a draw with top-ranked competition favourites the Netherlands, the previous day. Although China needed just one point to progress, it proved too big a mountain to climb. The Black Sticks surged to a 3-0 win to end China's Olympic dream, confirming that Team GB would indeed meet Spain in the last eight.

New Zealand's victory and subsequent elimination of China brought the pool phase to a close and revealed a quarter-final line-up that was intriguing and completely unexpected. As well as the head-to-head between Team GB and Spain, Pool B's second-placed finishers USA would face a tricky tie against Germany, who finished third in Pool A.

For the teams that finished third and fourth in Pool B, the challenge to keep their Olympic title hopes alive was arguably even tougher. Australia had ended their Pool B campaign in third place and were now destined for a quarter-final battle with Oceania adversaries New Zealand, who claimed second place in Pool A. For Champions Trophy winners Argentina, the news was even worse. Their shock fourth-place finish in Pool B meant that they would now face a monumental battle with Pool A winners the Netherlands, the team that defeated them for Olympic gold at London 2012.

By finishing ahead of the higher-ranked Argentina and Australia, and claiming the top two positions in Pool B, Team GB and USA had caused complete and utter chaos to the quarter-final line-up. Not only had they avoided meetings with the form teams from Pool A, they had also forced the four highest ranked teams on the planet to go toe-to-toe at the earliest possible stage. It was a fascinating scenario, one that would result in the elimination of two of hockey's powerhouse nations before the competition had even reached the semi-final phase. The importance of topping the pool was certainly not lost on Georgie Twigg, who described it as a huge relief.

'Finishing first was absolutely massive. We knew that if we could get that top spot we would play a slightly lesser side in the quarter-finals. With the margins at that level of hockey being so small, we knew it was so important. For USA, their defeat against us meant that they had a very tough game against the Germans, whereas for us we ended up facing Spain. We all knew how important that first-place finish was, and the relief when Alex (Danson) scored that last goal against the Americans was unbelievable. If a camera had been focussed on the bench at that time it would have seen everyone celebrating! We talked a lot about keeping our momentum going. We wanted to go into that quarter-final on a roll. Sometimes a loss can shake a team up a little bit, so it was great to be going into the quarter-final phase with the confidence sky high.'

As well as the quarter-final line-up, Team GB's route to the final was also known. Victory over Spain's Red Sticks would set up a semi-final meeting with the winner of the Oceania derby between Australia and New Zealand. While the Team GB squad were focussed solely on how they would overcome quarter-final opponents Spain, the fact that their route to the gold medal match would not be hampered by hot favourites the Netherlands or world number two Argentina had not gone unnoticed. It was a topic of great interest for Team GB's hockey fans but, according to team manager Karen Brown, was not something that the team paid any attention to at the time.

'We knew from our experiences at London 2012 that winning the pool and keeping our momentum going was more important than trying to plan for who you might play. This is not controllable by us and just uses up too much emotional energy, for staff as well as athletes. Our philosophy and process throughout the whole tournament was simple. One game at a time, and find a way to win that game.'

While things were looking rosy for Team GB's women's hockey team, the same could not be said for their male counterparts. The side coached by former international Bobby Crutchley and captained by Barry Middleton, England and Great Britain's record caps holder, had arrived in Rio with high expectations but had endured a torrid campaign, culminating in a 1-1 draw against Spain that effectively ended any hopes of a place in the quarter-finals. It was a shattering situation for everyone involved. 'Having been around the group since the end of the match, there is absolute devastation among both the players and management,' Great Britain Hockey chief operating officer Sally Munday said at the time. 'They work so hard, I see them all the time at Bisham Abbey, how hard they work and the life choices they make to be the best they can be. This isn't down to lack of preparation or lack of effort, this is a group of committed athletes who came here wanting to fulfil

Giselle Ansley on the move.
Koen Suyk

Last moments before the quarter-final match gets underway.
Koen Suyk

their Olympic dream and get on the medal podium, but it hasn't happened for them. Sometimes it is just not meant to be.'

With a strong camaraderie between the athletes and the staff of both Team GB hockey teams competing in Rio, it could be assumed that the struggles of the men could have been an unwanted, yet completely understandable, distraction for the women's group. Not so, according to Georgie Twigg, despite her own direct connection to the men's squad through her relationship with boyfriend and defender Iain Lewers.

'To be honest, it really didn't affect us. Initially, we hardly saw the men because we were playing on alternate days, and I hardly watched any of the men's matches because we may have had meetings, or were eating and generally sticking to our routine. Before the tournament Danny (Kerry) had told us that at events in the past we would occasionally go and watch the men or plan meetings around when the men were playing. However, we were not going to be doing that in Rio. He knew that some of us had ties with the men's team, but he made it clear that we were in Rio to do a job. Occasionally we might get the chance to watch half a game before going to dinner, but we did not change our schedule or routines to watch them. We were really

disappointed for the men, but at the same time, the way Iain dealt with it was to throw himself into watching the women and supporting the team by coming to our matches with my family.'

While Spain had ruined Team GB men's hopes of securing a first Olympic medal since Seoul 1988, the women were determined not to suffer the same fate against the Spanish opposition. The Team GB women had arrived in Brazil feeling optimistic about their chances, but thanks to the extra confidence and belief gained from five successive victories, that positivity had moved onto an entirely new level. However, with Team GB men now out of the running, there was a potential knock-on effect for the women. Prior to Rio 2016, UK Sport – the nation's high performance agency – had given Team GB's hockey teams a target of securing at least one medal in Rio, and failure to achieve this goal could seriously impact the funding of the British teams going into the next four-year cycle towards the Tokyo 2020 Olympic Games. So, did the group feel any additional pressure because of this worrying development?

'We never discussed it, either with the athletes or indeed within the women's management team,' said Karen Brown. 'After the quarter-final, I do recall Danny (Kerry), Craig (Keegan, assistant coach) and myself

Anthems and handshakes ahead of the fight for an Olympic semi-final berth.
Koen Suyk

expressing relief that we would make the top four and the ramifications of that with UK Sport but, to be honest, all talk about future funding is just noise and pressure, and you simply wouldn't want to add to the mix. The pressure of the quarter-final match is enough on its own.'

Monday 15 August 2016 was women's quarter-final day in Rio. Despite Team GB not being in action until the third game of the day, British hockey fans were keeping a close eye on the outcome of the first fixture. With the winner of the Oceania derby match providing Team GB's opponents should they make it to the semi-

finals, it was not without good reason. The grudge-match went to form, with Pool A runners-up New Zealand proving too strong for their Australian rivals as they claimed a 4-2 victory. It was the second Olympic Games in succession that the Black Sticks had reached the semi-final stage and the promise of a potential rematch against Team GB, the side that denied them the bronze medal at London 2012, was one that they would relish.

The USA versus Germany quarter-final was the second match of the day and certainly did not stick to script, with 'Die Danas' upsetting the world rankings and the form book to record a stunning victory over the

Spain's Red Sticks nervously wait for their encounter with Team GB.
Koen Suyk

Maddie Hinch receives applause on the occasion of her 100th international appearance ahead of the Olympic quarter-final meeting with Spain.
Koen Suyk

Breakthrough – Georgie Twigg gives Team GB an early lead against Spain's Red Sticks.
Koen Suyk

Players listen intently to the thoughts of Susannah Townsend.
Koen Suyk

Pan American champions. The fifth-ranked Americans came into the match having claimed 12 points in Pool B compared to Germany's seven in Pool A, but the team placed ninth in the world rankings were deserving winners and starting to look like serious title contenders.

Germany's against-the-odds triumph provided a stark reminder that anything can happen in the knock-out stages and that, despite being the form team, Team GB had to keep their standards as high as possible to overcome a Spanish team that had produced some excellent displays in Rio. For the second successive match, Danny Kerry would face a team coached by a fellow Englishman, with former U-21 international Adrian Lock having worked wonders with the group, since taking charge in 2013. Lock had introduced the Red Sticks women to a completely new playing philosophy and training programme, and the results were beginning to show. Although the youthful side were not likely to peak until Tokyo 2020 rather than in Rio, Kerry knew that Lock's Spain were well organised, extremely fit and their confidence was rising rapidly.

Despite the unwelcome disruption of a huge forest fire breaking out on the hills overlooking the Deodoro Hockey Centre just two hours before the start of the match, Team GB set about the task of reaching the Olympic semi-finals with ruthless professionalism. Kerry's team were simply irresistible in the first two quarters, with attacker Sophie Bray proving almost unplayable as she inspired her side into a deserved 3-0 half-time lead. Bray's constant willingness to direct her lightning speed and mesmerising skills at the Spanish defensive line provided a constant headache, winning penalty corners seemingly at will for her side. Georgie

Twigg wheels away in celebration.
Koen Suyk

Hollie Webb recovers possession for Team GB.
Frank Uijlenbroek

Twigg needed just eight minutes to open the scoring when she deflected Giselle Ansley's penalty corner pass into the roof of the Spanish goal, with Helen Richardson-Walsh doubling the advantage with a simple close range finish after more excellent work from Bray. The British dominance continued throughout the second quarter, with Lily Owsley making it 3-0 when she tapped in a perfect pass from Alex Danson to effectively kill the game at the half-way stage.

Although the Red Sticks improved in the third and fourth quarters, finding a route to goal was not proving easy. Maddie Hinch, playing her 100th international match, denied Spain's Begonia Garcia's close range effort before Owsley showed that she was just as effective in defence as in attack when she blocked Lola Reira's penalty corner strike. Spain edged closer to reducing the deficit when Berta Bonastre crashed her shot against the frame of the goal at the end of the third quarter, but Team GB's three-goal advantage would remain intact until seven minutes from the end. Georgina Oliva scored a fine solo goal to ruin Hinch's hopes of a third clean sheet at Rio, but it would prove to be only a consolation as Team GB reached the Olympic semi-finals for the second Games in succession, much to the delight of coach Kerry.

'In the first half we absolutely creamed them and then the second half it gets a bit wobbly,' said the tactician, speaking to Great Britain Hockey's media team. 'That's high performance sport and it's just whether you find a way through that. As much as I'd love to play an entire game the way we did in the first half, the reality is sport doesn't work like that and you have to find a way. I'm very proud. Our defence was strong when

Sam Quek sends a pass forwards.
Frank Uijlenbroek

it needed to be and we were just superb in the first half.'

Captain Kate Richardson-Walsh echoed Kerry's assessment. 'It was a dominant performance. We started brilliantly in the first five minutes, we really went at them. We created chances and had a corner and that really settled us down.

'Our form reminds me of the Olympic qualifiers in Valencia,' continued Kate, referring to the Hockey World League Semi-Final event in 2015 where Great Britain won all seven of their matches to seal their place at Rio 2016. 'We built momentum game to game and we went unbeaten at that tournament. It feels the same as that. We don't expect to win. We believe. We go back to square one for the next game. We can't go into the New Zealand game thinking emotionally. We believe we can get a medal but it's off in the distance and we are focused on the semi-final.'

Looking back on the fixture, Team GB assistant coach Craig Keegan described the Spain contest as arguably their trickiest game. 'We had played them

Shona McCallin beats Spain's captain Rocio Ybarra to the ball.

Frank Uijlenbroek

Players and coaching staff offer their thanks to the friends, family and Team GB supporters in the crowd.
Frank Uijlenbroek

Hollie Webb, Shona McCallin and Craig Keegan acknowledge the support from the spectators.
Frank Uijlenbroek

The players rejoice as Team GB seal a place in the semi-finals.
Frank Uijlenbroek

probably ten times in the previous 12 months. They knew us as well as anybody so we were pleased to get through that one.'

While the players could now rest knowing that they had taken another giant leap towards the medals, media attention switched onto a contest that ahead of Rio 2016 many had predicted would be the gold medal match. The Netherlands versus Argentina quarter-final was a classic and, despite finishing fourth in Pool B, Las Leonas produced easily their best performance of the competition. Sadly, it was not quite good enough to deny the Beijing 2008 and London 2012 Olympic gold medallists their place in the final four. The Dutch ran out 3-2 winners, avenging their Champions Trophy Final defeat seven weeks earlier and moving Oranje to within two victories of claiming a record-breaking third successive Olympic gold medal. It was an emotional end to the competition for Argentina, whose long wait for their first Olympic gold medal goes on.

Quarter-Final results - 15 August 2016

New Zealand	**4-2**	**Australia**
Anita McLaren 7m PC		Kathryn Slattery
Kelsey Smith 24m PC		33m PC, 59m FG
Gemma Flynn 39m FG		
Olivia Merry 43m FG		

USA	**1-2**	**Germany**
Katelyn Falgowski 57m FG		Marie Mävers 8m FG
		Lisa Altenburg 14m FG

Team GB	**3-1**	**Spain**
Georgie Twigg 8m PC		Georgina Oliva 53m FG
Helen Richardson-Walsh		
13m FG		
Lily Owsley 27m FG		

Netherlands	**3-2**	**Argentina**
Lidewij Welten 5m FG		Florencia Habif 41m PC
Laurien Leurink 25m FG		Delfina Merino 53m PC
Kelly Jonker 37m PC		

Semi-Final line-up

17 August: Netherlands v Germany
17 August: New Zealand v Team GB

Team huddle.
Koen Suyk

Chapter 8
The Semi-Finals

Team GB and New Zealand's Black Sticks prepare for action, with a place in the Olympic final up for grabs.
Frank Uijlenbroek

Not even the Netherlands, the red-hot favourites and reigning Olympic and world champions, had managed to achieve a six-match winning run en route to the women's hockey semi-finals of the Rio 2016 Olympic Games – drawing with New Zealand in their third pool match. In form and now very much at the business end of the competition, attention from the media and the watching British public on Danny Kerry's side intensified dramatically.

Team GB's displays prior to reaching the semi-finals had turned plenty of heads, but this was something different entirely. With sports broadcasters, journalists, celebrities and fans all speculating about the possibilities of Kate Richardson-Walsh and her squad going all the way to the gold medal, the performances of the women's hockey team had caught the attention of the nation.

As well as her remarkable goalkeeping performances on the field, Maddie Hinch had been

attracting plenty of new fans thanks to her column on the BBC Sport website. Due to the squad's collective decision to stay away from social media, it provided a glimpse inside the bubble as they progressed along their Olympic journey.

'With games back-to-back, there's basically no time to train,' wrote Hinch after her side's 3-0 pool victory over India. 'We've been to Team GB House to use the pool and the gym, but not out on the training pitch. In tournaments in the past, I would normally train on the pitch the day after a quiet game like India, but going back a year or so I stopped doing that so that I was better able to adapt if there was a longer distance to the training pitch in Rio. We've changed my whole routine because it would help us out here, that's the level of detail our coaches and staff go to in preparation for an Olympics. We've trained ourselves to not need specific facilities and it works.'

With excellent form, soaring confidence levels and a groundswell of support from fans and media, it seemed to onlookers that something special was happening within the women's hockey team. Team GB were on course for a record haul of medals in Rio, and with Danny Kerry's team now in the semi-finals, hopes were high that hockey could make a golden contribution to that tally. However, back in the bubble, normal service was still very much in place.

'From the outside I am sure it looked special and amazing, especially with the media coverage,' said assistant coach and team manager Karen Brown. 'However, from the inside it was more like: this is what we do, this is what we train for – to win hockey matches. As far as we saw it, this was what we had planned and trained for. We did the same in Valencia at the Olympic qualifier and nearly went through all of 2015 without losing a game. At the time we really didn't realise how special, how magical it all appeared to people back home.'

Laura Unsworth puts her all into a pass.
Frank Uijlenbroek

Hannah Macleod bursts forward.
Frank Uijlenbroek

While Karen Brown and the team may not have been aware of the frenzy that was building back home, they could not avoid the excitement shown by their fellow Team GB representatives, who were all too willing to express their support in the Athletes' Village when the opportunity arose.

'The tennis player Jamie Murray has been really hooked on the hockey, I was chatting to him in the physio room,' wrote Hinch in her BBC Sport blog. 'The hockey is doing well to get people excited. We're getting a fan-base and it seems the Murray brothers are top of the list.

Becky James, the cyclist, said to me the matches were brilliant and she wished us good luck. It's a great sport to watch, as a group we always talk about inspiring people to get involved with the sport. I was also reliably informed that Jean-Claude Van Damme "liked" a Tweet from GB Hockey to the BBC, so the sport is getting bigger!'

If people had not been inspired by their performances leading up to the semi-finals, they certainly were after what proved to be a bruising semi-final clash with New Zealand's Black Sticks – a team high on confidence after their quarter-final success over trans-

Georgie Twigg erupts with glee as Alex Danson
opens the scoring against New Zealand.
Frank Uijlenbroek

Tasman rivals Australia. 'New Zealand are a very fast side,' said Danny Kerry ahead of the contest. 'They've got a lot of pace and a lot of good goalscorers. It will be a hell of a game.'

Those comments were echoed at the time by Team GB defender Crista Cullen, who recognised the need to remain solid at the back but also exploit what she saw as a chink in the Black Sticks' armour. 'New Zealand play a very attacking style, which is great because it opens it up and gives gaps to attack into. We've shown a lot of resilience defensively – typically British defending – and we need to bring that out in the next game.

'We can't get carried away as it's a totally new group to four years ago, and with that is a totally new ethos and approach,' continued the

triple Olympian, referring to comparisons made to the GB side that beat the Black Sticks to the bronze medal at London 2012. 'Every game we've come out with our business hats on to just get it done.'

Team GB's showdown with New Zealand took place on the evening of Wednesday 17 August 2016, a few hours after women's semi-final day kicked off with a clash between great European rivals the Netherlands and Germany. The top-ranked Dutch may have beaten the ninth-ranked Germans 2-0 in their Pool A meeting earlier in the competition, but were given a stern test by a team determined to reclaim the Olympic title that they won at Athens 2004. Germany surprised with a first-quarter goal from Lisa Schütze, before legendary Dutch captain Maartje Paumen levelled matters with a trademark

Team-mates rush to congratulate Alex Danson after she scores against New Zealand.
Frank Uijlenbroek

penalty corner early in the second period. Remarkably, that scoreline remained unchanged for the rest of the match, meaning that the contest would be decided by a shootout.

A nervy shootout competition saw only four of the ten takers convert their chances, locking the score at 2-2 and initiating 'sudden death'. Following successful efforts from Germany captain Janne Müller-Wieland and Willemijn Bos of the Netherlands, the match was settled when Marie Mävers was denied by Dutch shot-stopper Joyce Sombroek before 2014 World Player of the Year Ellen Hoog scored to put Holland into their fourth Olympic final in succession. The favourites were now one win away from claiming a third Olympic gold medal on the bounce – an unprecedented feat in women's hockey.

It was going to take a monumental effort to stop the mighty Dutch, but both the players of Team GB and New Zealand had plenty of reasons to believe that the world number one side were not invincible. The British squad was crammed full of players who had beaten the Netherlands to European gold with England in 2015, while the Black Sticks had matched their illustrious opponents with a deserved draw in the pool phase. In truth, the gold medal game could not have been further from the thoughts of the Team GB players. As always, their concentration was on nothing other than the task in hand – beating the Black Sticks, something they achieved with their most devastating display of the competition.

Danny Kerry's team played with a level of intensity and physicality that New Zealand found hard to handle, pressurising the opposition defence and forcing

Georgie Twigg is attended by Team GB's Emma Batchelor during the semi-final clash with New Zealand.
Frank Uijlenbroek

frequent errors. This was Kerry's Team GB at their best, with each player knowing their precise role to execute the game plan whilst simultaneously denying the Black Sticks an opportunity to implement their own.

Despite being out-muscled and out-manoeuvred for long periods, the New Zealanders certainly had their chances but failed to show that all-important killer touch in front of goal, a talent that Team GB striker Alex Danson has always had in abundance. Danson showed her striker's instinct in the 22nd minute to open the scoring with a classic poacher's goal, picking up the pieces to force home from close range a split second after Black Sticks goalkeeper Sally Rutherford had blocked Crista Cullen's penalty corner drag-flick.

Moments after taking the lead, Maddie Hinch was forced to prove her worth yet again when she

A mouth injury sees Georgie Twigg join Cullen in the treatment room, with both athletes returning to the action soon after.
Frank Uijlenbroek

Team GB discuss their options with the match tentatively poised at 1-0.
Frank Uijlenbroek

denied Gemma Flynn with an instinctive save with her right foot, while New Zealand's all-time leading goal-scorer Anita McLaren gave Team GB a warning that the contest was far from over with a penalty corner drag-flick that travelled just wide of the mark on the brink of half-time.

New Zealand continued their search for a leveller in the third quarter, but found themselves up against a team playing with exceptional discipline. As she had done throughout her career, Kate Richardson-Walsh was leading by example, marshalling her defensive line with military precision, putting her body on the line to make vital tackles to keep the Black Sticks at bay. While captain Kate impressed, Crista Cullen and Georgie Twigg both exhibited a jaw-dropping level of courageousness. Cullen was forced to leave the field with blood pouring from her head onto the blue artificial turf after smashing into an opponent's knee, with Twigg

joining her in the treatment room just minutes later when the ball flew into her mouth.

Cullen remembers the moment Twigg appeared in the treatment room with absolute clarity. 'When she walked in my immediate reaction was to tell (team doctor) Mike Rossiter to stitch me up faster so I could get back out there. My first thought was that it was messing up our player rotation strategy. I needed to make sure that those players who were out there having to cover the injured players could get off, get some rest and get some fluids on board. So yes, as soon as she walked in I immediately started pushing the medical staff to hurry up. I think it is standard for hockey players. It is the nature of what we do, especially as defenders. I was fine, I just needed to have a few stitches and get back out onto the pitch so I could do my job for the team.'

Georgie Twigg's recollections of the situation were equally vivid. 'My first thought after the ball hit me

Key moment as Helen Richardson-Walsh is felled before converting the subsequent penalty stroke. Worryingly, she then left the field injured.
Frank Uijlenbroek

Helen Richardson-Walsh celebrates
after scoring from the penalty spot.
Frank Uijlenbroek

was that I had broken my jaw, like Kate (Richardson-Walsh) had done in London 2012. I was taken to the changing room to see our doctor, who was stitching Crista up at that time, so I had to lie on the second physio bed. The dentist checked my teeth and they were fine, and then Crista went out to rejoin the match and Mike came to see me. It was all rather eventful! Although I needed stitches on the inside of my mouth, I was so lucky because there was a moment where I thought that was it, you know? I was quite shaken up by it, if I'm honest. Still, I ran back out to the pitch, secretly hoping that the game was nearly over and that we had won only to find that it was still only 1-0 and that we still had ages left! At one point we had Sam Quek (defender) on the forward line, so everyone was like "Twiggy, get back out there and get Sam back in defence"!'

The astonishing bravery of Cullen and Twigg stirred social media into a frenzy, with people expressing their disbelief at the lengths those athletes were prepared to go to in search of glory for their nation whilst also recognising that hockey was dynamic, action-packed and, occasionally, utterly brutal.

Team GB's resolve was rewarded with 12 minutes of the match remaining. Helen Richardson-Walsh burst through on goal only to be brought down by Black Sticks captain Kayla Whitelock, resulting in a penalty stroke and a yellow card five-minute suspension for the New Zealander. Rather gingerly, the felled Richardson-Walsh got to her feet and coolly doubled Team GB's lead from the spot. It proved to be her final contribution to the contest, immediately limping off the pitch with what seemed like a side effect from the collision with Whitelock. The converted penalty was a knockout blow for New Zealand, who quickly conceded another stroke after great work from Lily Owsley. With Helen Richardson-Walsh watching on from the sidelines, Alex Danson took responsibility for the penalty and made absolutely no mistake, sealing a 3-0 victory and putting Team GB's

Helen Richardson-Walsh goes down injured immediately after converting her crucial penalty stroke.
It was to be her last contribution to the game, raising concerns about her prospects of competing in the gold medal match.
Frank Uijlenbroek

Alex Danson seals Team GB's place in the final, converting from the penalty spot to claim her second goal of the match.

Frank Uijlenbroek

women into their first Olympic final. They had done it the hard way and certainly had the casualties to prove it, but it was a result that was richly deserved and had delighted head coach Danny Kerry.

'They executed brilliantly today,' Kerry told Great Britain Hockey's media team immediately after the contest. 'They absolutely played how they'd been set out to do it and it really paid dividends. I was really proud of them playing under pressure in the second half. They kept playing forward trying to take opportunities and I'm really proud of that. That makes us the most successful GB women's team ever at an Olympics. But there's still one more game to go and they're going to keep their feet on the ground.'

He continued: 'Holland in the final – they've probably got a bit of a point to prove after the England team and the Europeans. I think it will be a tight, cagey affair. They have some talented players and they will probably start as red-hot favourites but we like it that way.'

Tears, pride and passion as Team GB celebrate reaching a first-ever Olympic final in women's hockey.
Frank Uijlenbroek

The hooter sounds and the celebrations begin.
Frank Uijlenbroek

John Hurst, Shona McCallin and Georgie Twigg celebrate.
Frank Uijlenbroek

Supporters show their delight at Team GB's performance.
Frank Uijlenbroek

Sam Quek admitted to journalist Rod Gilmour, writing for *The Evening Standard*, that the way the team had reached the gold medal match had left her in a state of shock. 'You saw it all out there. Two of our girls hit and drawing blood and we still got it going. We are tight, we are solid and we are definitely out to get that gold.'

'I'm over the moon,' said Helen Richardson-Walsh before reassuringly suggesting her injury was a bad case of cramp rather than anything more serious, which came as good news ahead of the gold medal match. After the Games, she revealed that it was actually a hamstring problem that had left her a serious doubt for the final. 'We've beaten a very, very good side pretty convincingly and we've got one more game. That's seven from seven, we want eight from eight.'

Semi-Final results – 17 August 2016

Netherlands   1-1   Germany

Netherlands		Germany
Maartje Paumen 16m PC		Lisa Schütze 11m PC
	Shootout	
Willemijn Bos – Goal	4-3	Janne Müller-Wieland – Goal
Ellen Hoog – No Goal		Marie Mävers – Goal
Marloes Keetels – No Goal		Lisa Altenburg – No Goal
Margot van Geffen – Goal		Jana Teschke – No Goal
Kelly Jonker – No Goal		Franzisca Hauke – No Goal
Willemijn Bos – Goal		Janne Müller-Wieland – Goal
Ellen Hoog - Goal		Marie Mävers - No Goal

New Zealand   0-3   Team GB

New Zealand		Team GB
		Alex Danson 22m PC, 52m PS
		Helen Richardson-Walsh 48m PS

Medal match line-up
Bronze medal match: Germany v New Zealand
Gold medal match: Netherlands v Team GB

Chapter 9
The Final

No matter the result of the gold medal game, Team GB's women's hockey team were now assured of a best ever finish at an Olympic Games. The famous bronze-medal-winning performances at Barcelona 1992 and on home soil at London 2012 some 20 years later were going to be eclipsed by either sparkling silver or glittering gold at Rio 2016.

While the collective hearts of Team GB hockey fans desperately hoped that the team would give legendary captain Kate Richardson-Walsh the fairy-tale ending that her remarkable international career deserved, their heads were taking a more rational, cautious approach. The Netherlands were overwhelming favourites for the title, meaning that Team GB were going to have to produce something extraordinary to stop the Dutch from becoming the first women's hockey team to win four Olympic gold medals and three successively.

Twelve years had passed since the Netherlands last suffered defeat in Olympic competition. A surprise loss at the hands of Germany in the final of the Athens 2004 Olympic Games was followed by two stunning triumphs, with Oranje storming to gold at Beijing 2008 and London 2012 before reaffirming their position as the greatest team on the planet by winning the Rabobank Hockey World Cup 2014 on home soil in The Hague.

The Dutch squad competing in Rio contained an almost embarrassment of riches. Shot-stopper Joyce Sombroek came into the event as a two-time winner of the International Hockey Federation's World Goalkeeper of the Year award, while attacking stars Naomi van As, Ellen Hoog and Lidewij Welten had all been crowned FIH

Team GB sing the national anthem ahead of their Olympic final showdown with the Netherlands, the tournament favourites.
Frank Uijlenbroek

Player of the Year on separate occasions between 2009 and 2015. While Sombroek, van As, Hoog and Welten were all capable of producing mesmerising moments of brilliance, there was still one Dutch player who, when it came to performing in the big games, was a cut above the rest.

In team captain Maartje Paumen, the FIH Player of the Year in 2011 and 2012, the Netherlands had

Orange shirts outnumbering British colours at the Olympic Hockey Centre.
Koen Suyk

one of hockey's most iconic figures and arguably the greatest exponent of the penalty corner drag-flick that the women's game has ever seen. Ahead of the Rio 2016 final, Paumen had scored 18 goals in 21 Olympic matches since debuting at Beijing 2008, making her the top women's goalscorer in Olympic history. If Team GB were going to win the gold, they would need to keep Paumen as quiet as possible.

As well as the talent on the field, there was also a considerable presence on the sidelines in the shape of head coach Alyson Annan, herself a two-time FIH Player of the Year winner and double Olympic gold medallist with Australia at the Atlanta 1996 and Sydney 2000 Olympic Games. The celebrated Hockeyroo stepped into the position vacated by previous head coach Sjoerd Marijne, who walked away in the summer of 2015

Maddie Hinch denies Dutch ace
Maartje Paumen from the penalty spot.
Frank Uijlenbroek

Hands held aloft, Hinch again shows why she is rated the best goalkeeper in the world.
Frank Uijlenbroek

Sophie Bray bursts into the Netherlands circle from the left to create the opening goal.
Frank Uijlenbroek

Maartje Paumen is distraught after Maddie Hinch saves from the penalty spot.
Koen Suyk

following the Netherlands' shock defeat at the hands of England in the final of the EuroHockey Championships. With so much quality and experience at their disposal both on and off the field, the reigning world champions had every reason to believe that they could re-write the record books in Rio.

While Danny Kerry's confident, tactically astute, battle-ready Team GB were sure to give the hot favourites a serious run for their money, whether it would be good enough to cause a repeat of England's stunning European success a year earlier remained to

be seen. There was absolutely no uncertainty in the minds of the players, however, as the much-discussed gold medal mentality came to the forefront once again. 'It's not luck that we're here,' said a bullish Lily Owsley, speaking to Jonathan Liew of *The Daily Telegraph* after the semi-final victory over New Zealand. 'It's not a fluke. We've put in the hard yards in the last few years, we've done our job and we've done the work, and that's why we've got here. We're not settling for silver.'

Like Owsley, Sam Quek was also confident about her side's ability to defeat the odds thanks to the never-say-die attitude that had been a symbol of the team's performances throughout their title challenge in Rio. 'Whether it's 60 minutes or one minute left, we just keep going and we will take it to the Dutch,' said Quek in conversation with EuroHockey.org. 'We know we can take Holland on and push them all the way. And if it is between heart, skill and passion – we have got it all. We know them inside out and have played them so many times. It's going to be a tight game and we will stay tight as a squad and have the talent all around the pitch to do the job.'

While the British girls were displaying never before seen levels of self-assurance, the Dutch gave hints that they were not entirely satisfied with their form. The shootout victory over ninth-ranked Germany in the semi-finals was far closer than many had predicted, with Dutch captain Paumen making it clear in no uncertain terms that the team needed to raise their game in order to win gold. Speaking to Rio2016.com immediately following the Germany match, double Olympic gold medallist Paumen said: 'We made it to the final now and the only thing we are here for is the gold medal, but we have to play better than this game today.'

Team GB's astounding seven-match winning record on their way to reaching the Olympic final had captured the nation's imagination, and the exploits of the women's hockey team were headline news. The brutal, blood-soaked triumph over New Zealand had earned them the admiration of the British public, who now wanted to see if these warriors could finish the job. The huge interest in the contest was reflected by Olympic host broadcaster the BBC, who committed to showing the gold medal match live and uninterrupted on their flagship channel BBC One, a move that was in part triggered by complaints from incensed British

Team GB spent much of the match defending against the world's number one side.
Frank Uijlenbroek

Lily Owsley and Helen Richardson-Walsh celebrate the opening goal.
Frank Uijlenbroek

Kitty van Male (centre) made no mistake with her finish, smashing a backhand strike into
the roof of the Team GB goal to level the scores at 1-1.
Koen Suyk

Crista Cullen roars with delight after her first ever open play strike in international hockey restores parity at 2-2.
Frank Uijlenbroek

Netherlands captain Maartje Paumen finally beats Maddie Hinch with a thunderous penalty corner strike catching everyone by surprise to give the Dutch a 2-1 lead.
Koen Suyk

sports fans who were forced to switch channels as the semi-final match with New Zealand was approaching its climax. It was a bold decision that would result in the delaying of the *Ten O'Clock News*, but one that would allow more than nine million people to witness a moment of British sporting history.

On the evening of Friday 19 August 2016, shortly after Germany had claimed the bronze medal with a 2-1 victory over New Zealand, a near capacity crowd had gathered at the Deodoro Hockey Stadium in anticipation of the showdown. The British fans were vastly outnumbered by the orange-clad supporters of the Netherlands, who had been joined by members of the Dutch Royal Family, with King Willem-Alexander, Queen Maxima and Princess Amalia all present for the occasion. Despite their numerical disadvantage, the British contingent made their voices heard throughout the most dramatic of games.

The Team GB fans had been boosted by the news that, thanks to the sterling work of Dr Mike Rossiter and physio Emma Batchelor, the injured trio of Crista Cullen, Georgie Twigg and Helen Richardson-Walsh had all recovered from the wounds sustained in the semi-final clash with New Zealand. It was a situation that, according to a reflective Cullen, was always going to be the case. 'To play in an Olympic final, I had never been lucky enough to do that,' said the defender, who was to play a crucial role in the contest. 'Even if I had limbs hanging off I would have done everything in my power to make sure I was able to get out there for 60 minutes and I'm sure everyone else would have done the same.'

The opening quarter of the match was played at a furious tempo, with Team GB battling in every section of the field to match their illustrious opponents. However, with just seven minutes played, disaster struck when defender Sam Quek tangled with Dutch midfielder Laurien Leurink and conceded a penalty stroke, providing Maartje Paumen with an early opportunity to make her mark. Paumen aimed her shot towards the roof of the British net, but Maddie Hinch read the situation and was quick to react, stepping to her right and palming the ball away to safety.

Team GB congratulate Cullen on her goal.
Frank Uijlenbroek

Team GB fans show their support.
Frank Uijlenbroek

Just two minutes after the Dutch had squandered their chance from the penalty spot, Team GB rubbed salt into the wound by taking a shock lead. Sophie Bray was the creator of the goal, powering into the circle from the left and showing super skills to evade numerous challenges before forcing a save from Netherlands shot-stopper Joyce Sombroek, with Lily Owsley on hand to bundle home the rebound and trigger scenes of jubilation from the British fans in the stadium.

That goal sparked a fierce reaction from the reigning champions, who laid siege to the Team GB goal in the latter stages of the opening quarter but could find no way past the inspired Hinch, who made another crucial save from Paumen to ensure that her side went into the break with their lead still intact.

The Netherlands were almost totally dominant in the second period, and got a deserved leveller within a minute of the restart. 2015 FIH Player of the Year Lidewij Welten forced Kate Richardson-Walsh into a rare mistake before bearing down on goal and supplying the perfect pass to Kitty van Male, who moved past the onrushing Hinch and fired a spectacular backhand strike into the roof of the net.

The British defence was forced to soak up immense pressure from the top-ranked Dutch and rode their luck at times, especially when a stunning shot from Naomi van As crashed against the crossbar. It came as no surprise when the second Dutch goal arrived in the 24th minute, although Paumen's 19th goal in Olympic competition was certainly unusual in its style. Having seen her world-renowned penalty corner drag-flicks being swatted away with consummate ease by Hinch, Paumen unleashed a rarely used weapon in her armoury, smashing a vicious strike into the bottom left corner of the Team GB goal. It was a brilliant tactical move from the Dutch captain, an old-school strategy that bamboozled the Team GB defence and gave the Netherlands a 2-1 lead.

It seemed that the Dutch had finally taken the game under their control, but Team GB were clearly not reading the script and hit back almost immediately. A searching pass forward from Giselle Ansley found its way through to defender Crista Cullen, who had somehow managed to sneak unnoticed into the Dutch scoring circle, where she was completely unmarked. Although Cullen's first-time slap-shot lacked power, it caught Dutch goalkeeper Joyce Sombroek off guard and unbalanced, and she watched helplessly as the

Kitty van Male scores her second goal of the game to put the Dutch back in front at 3-2.
Frank Uijlenbroek

Dutch fans watch on as their side move into a 3-2 lead.
Frank Uijlenbroek

ball looped over her outstretched right leg before
hitting the backboard. Cullen let out a primal roar as she
wheeled away in celebration, before racing back to
the defensive line to ensure that Team GB's gold medal
dream remained very much alive going into half-time.

For Team GB assistant coach and goalscoring
trainer Craig Keegan, Cullen's strike – her first ever open
play goal in international hockey despite an impressive
record from penalty corner situations – was a magical
moment. 'It was brilliant for so many reasons: It was
taken first time, which I always encourage the players to
do; she was a back three player who was in our circle,
so she had followed the play upfield, which we were
encouraging them to do. Yes, it was a slight mis-hit but
what is important for me is that it is not always about
the contact, it is about the ability to take it early and
get the ball on target. The goalkeeper kicked over the
top of it so maybe it wasn't the best goalkeeping, but a
defender in the circle, a first-time shot – it all caused the
keeper a problem.'

Nicola White (centre) forces the ball home from close range to level the match for a third time.
Frank Uijlenbroek

Cullen remembers the moment with relish. 'I only ever score corners and I don't really know what I was doing in their circle. Even the coach asked me at the end of the match what I was doing up there. It was just one of those situations where you weigh up risk against opportunity and I decided to go into the space. It wasn't the most clinical of finishes but I'll take it any day of the week, scoring in the Olympic final.'

Team GB again found themselves on the back foot in the third quarter, repelling wave after wave of high paced Dutch attacks before eventually conceding a third. Kitty van Male was again the scorer, finishing off a wonderfully worked penalty corner routine to leave Team GB trailing 3-2 going into a tense and dramatic fourth and final period.

While the Netherlands continued to dominate, their opponents were doing everything in their power to keep the contest alive. With eight minutes remaining, Team GB's chance arrived in the shape of their first penalty corner of the match. It was an opportunity that

Netherlands coach and legendary Australian international Alyson Annan offers words of encouragement to her team.
Koen Suyk

Team GB show their fighting spirit whilst congratulating White on her crucial goal.
Frank Uijlenbroek

Sophie Bray fouled in the shootout by goalkeeper Joyce Sombroek, leading to a penalty stroke dispatched by Helen Richardson-Walsh.
Koen Suyk

they would not waste, with the Dutch defenders denying two shots before Nicola White forced the ball over the goal-line to restore parity yet again.

White's strike proved to be the last goal of an astonishing final, meaning that the destination of the Olympic gold medal would be decided by a shootout. For 60 minutes, Team GB had withstood everything that the world's most feared attacking side had thrown at them and somehow emerged on the other side on level terms. Now it was all down to who could hold their nerve in the most pressurised of sporting environments, where every moment had the potential to either win or lose the greatest prize in sport. However, thanks to England's shootout victory over the Dutch at the European Championships 12 months earlier, the British girls knew that they had the psychological edge. They also had an extraordinary goalkeeper.

Maddie Hinch was the superstar of the shootout at the Euros, conceding just one goal as England denied the Netherlands what would have been a ninth European crown in 12 editions of the competition. Ahead of that shootout, Hinch was seen studying a notebook which contained detailed information she

Margot van Geffen is forced wide by Team GB goalkeeper Maddie Hinch before seeing her shot bounce off the post and away to safety, giving Hollie Webb the chance to seal the gold medal.
Koen Suyk

Hollie Webb stays cool as she seeks to win gold for Team GB.
Frank Uijlenbroek

had gathered to understand how each player might attempt to beat her in the eight seconds that they had to find the back of the net.

Prior to the shootout in Rio, Hinch was again seen consulting her notebook. As expected, she had done her homework, having spent hours with Team GB's video analysts watching back footage of the Dutch shootout victory over Germany in the semi-final. 'It is never easy facing back-to-back shootouts,' said assistant coach Karen Brown. 'That would have unsettled the Dutch for sure.'

Against Germany, the Dutch, by necessity, partially revealed their hand, and Hinch took full advantage to learn as much about the players she was likely to face as she could in a bid to achieve the best possible outcome. Hinch's preparation was meticulous, to the point where even her drinks container featured some helpful pointers. Written on a strip of cloth tape stuck to the side of her Team GB branded water bottle, Hinch reminded herself to "RELAX", keep her "HANDS UP", to "CHILL OUT" and to "STAY BIG".

While Hinch had formulated her own game-plan for the one-on-ones, she had little control over what her team-mates might do when they came up against the imposing figure of Joyce Sombroek, the brilliant Dutch goalkeeper who excelled in her side's success in the semi-final. With arguably the two best goalkeepers in the world on show, the attacking players on both teams found goals hard to come by when the shootout got underway. Team GB's Helen Richardson-Walsh and Willemijn Bos of the Netherlands were both denied by superb saves, with Alex Danson and Ellen Hoog suffering the same fate to leave the score at 0-0 after two rounds.

Team GB midfielder Georgie Twigg, who was not named as one of the shootout takers, recalls her memories of watching things unfold. 'I remember us all standing in a line with arms around each other and, as someone who has often been one of the shootout takers, I recall thinking "Goodness, this is even worse to watch". We are a very superstitious bunch, so we were all trying to do the same things that had helped us win the matches leading up to the final. I did a little fist pump when Maddie saved the first one, and sticking with the superstition I had to carry on doing the same thing for every single attempt! It was all about trying to stay calm. I remember when the match finished with the score at

Hollie Webb sends her
shootout effort inside the
right post before erupting
with joy.
Frank Uijlenbroek

Hollie Webb is lost in a sea of British players as the gold medal celebrations truly begin.
Frank Uijlenbroek

3-3, Kate (Richardson-Walsh) sprinted over to the bench and said "yep, we've got this girls", and it was how we were all feeling ahead of the shootout. We weren't jumping up and down but we were confident, certainly compared to the Dutch.'

The crucial breakthrough came in round three when Sombroek mistimed her attempted tackle on Sophie Bray and brought the Briton crashing to the ground. A penalty stroke was awarded, with Helen Richardson-Walsh shaking off the disappointment of her earlier miss by finding the bottom corner to give Team GB a crucial 1-0 lead. It was an advantage that would soon be reinforced by more brilliance from Hinch, who channelled Laurien Leurink away from goal before making a stunning save to deflect the Dutch player's shot wide of the target.

Laura Unsworth was next up for Team GB, but Sombroek was not to be beaten, blocking a slap-shot from the top of the circle with Unsworth's second effort sailing over the crossbar. Sombroek was doing her best to keep the Netherlands alive, but her team were running out of opportunities and now needed Margot van Geffen to score if the outcome of the match was to remain in their hands. Yet again, Hinch – now trending on Twitter – would keep the Dutch off the scoreboard, forcing her challenger wide to cut down the scoring angle. It had the desired effect, with Van Geffen's low shot rebounding off the near post before being booted

away to safety by the Team GB custodian. It was a moment that Hinch clearly enjoyed, raising her hands to her team-mates knowing that they were now just one goal away from achieving something truly magnificent.

The responsibility of Team GB's fifth and final shootout would fall onto the shoulders of defender Hollie Webb, and she was not about to let the opportunity slide. Driving towards goal, Webb was calmness personified, finding the space between Sombroek and the right post to hit the back of the net and spark scenes of wild celebration amongst the Team GB squad, not to mention their army of loyal fans in the Deodoro Hockey Stadium and the millions of Britons watching on television. Against all the odds, Team GB had found a way to win yet again, and an extraordinary gold medal success was theirs.

'I don't think I can really put it into words yet,' said a clearly shocked Hollie Webb after the game. 'It hasn't really sunk in. I don't really know what's happened. I'm just so proud of all the girls that played tonight. I'm so proud to be British. So proud to be a part of Team GB. If that just inspired anyone to pick up a hockey stick, any age, any gender, anyone can get involved, then our job has been done.'

'We know we're good at shootouts,' said a thrilled Danny Kerry. 'We have some tough competitors and probably the best goalie in the world in shootouts. As soon as it went there I knew we would win.'

Assistant coaches Craig Keegan and Karen Brown share an embrace, knowing that the job was done.
Frank Uijlenbroek

Shootout heroes Maddie Hinch and Hollie Webb.
Frank Uijlenbroek

The newly-crowned Olympic champions pose for the photographers.
Frank Uijlenbroek

Giselle Ansley enjoys a victory lap of the Olympic Hockey Centre.
Frank Uijlenbroek

For Kate Richardson-Walsh, the dream ending to her international career had come true. 'It feels ridiculously amazing – I don't think it will ever sink in, what we have achieved,' said the retiring captain, who days later would be named Team GB's Flag Bearer for the Closing Ceremony of the Rio 2016 Olympic Games. 'It was a fairytale ending to an incredible few weeks in Rio, the culmination of years and years of hard work. I've seen each and every one of those girls who stood on that podium go through some very hard times over the years, and to see them all just beaming, having achieved their dream after everything they have been through just makes me immensely proud.'

The emotions of the gold medal success proved to be too much for Mel Clewlow, Kate's former England

and Great Britain team-mate, who commentated on the final for the BBC. 'I had to apologise to viewers and turn my microphone off when trying to sum up as realisation kicked in as to what they had just achieved,' said the Beijing 2008 Olympian. 'Yes, I was there as a commentator but at that moment I think my emotions spoke for pretty much every hockey fan in Britain and that's also how I see myself.

'I have said many times in commentary that Danny Kerry is the best tactical coach I have ever worked with. Every single player goes into each game knowing exactly what is expected of them. I don't think GB had the most talented individual players, but Danny and his coaching team certainly had the best and most consistent team at Rio.

Medals around their necks, Team GB sing the national anthem.
Koen Suyk

'For someone like Kate, who I class as a friend and someone I played with for such a long time, to finish a remarkable career with an Olympic gold medal was an emotional moment. You could see exactly what it meant to her when she was standing on the podium. It was written all over her face.'

Chapter 10

Inspiring the Future

Twelve years after their devastating failure to qualify for the Athens 2004 Olympic Games, Team GB's women were the Olympic hockey champions. It was a monumental achievement, the enormity of which was not lost on long-serving midfielder Helen Richardson-Walsh.

'It is difficult to put into words what this means, and I am struggling to believe it,' said Helen, speaking to the BBC the morning after the greatest night of her sporting life. 'Seventeen years ago when I started my career we were so far off. We have put in so much hard work, grown and grown over the last eight years. We have got an incredible group of players and staff and we had the belief. It just means absolutely everything to get this gold medal.'

Helen's sentiments were echoed by captain Kate Richardson-Walsh, who also revealed the joy of watching her wife achieve her lifelong ambition after overcoming numerous injury setbacks. 'To see Helen go through

A new generation of hockey heroes soak up the atmosphere after a gold medal success that would prove life-changing for all involved.
Frank Uijlenbroek

double back surgery, the strength and resilience she has shown resonates through the whole squad. It honestly and truly comes from every single person. Everyone who touches this squad has it and it is infectious. We wanted to be the difference, create history and inspire the future and we have done it.'

The two players had earned their happy ending, becoming Britain's first married couple to win an Olympic gold medal since Cyril and Dorothy Wright secured victory in the sailing at the Antwerp 1920 Olympic Games. It was, Kate admitted cheerily, time to step away from the international game. 'This is it, 100 per cent. We are going to retire as reigning Olympic champions and it is a good way to go out.'

While the long international careers of the Richardson-Walshes may have ended – Helen had not officially confirmed her retirement at the time of publication – their well deserved time in the limelight was only just beginning. The media coverage of the bronze medal at London 2012 had proven a mere appetiser to the kind of attention that comes hand in hand with winning an Olympic gold medal.

In the days that followed their stunning hockey gold medal triumph, the Team GB women's hockey players emerged from their Olympic bubble to find themselves in the eye of a hurricane. Imagery of the celebrations immediately following Hollie Webb's winner in the shootout were given star billing across the British media, with the team featuring on both the front and back pages of the national newspapers. The success had left a lasting impression on the watching British public, who in the days immediately following the Games took to the BBC website to vote the triumph as their favourite British moment of Rio 2016. The profile of the team had never been higher, and the naming of Kate Richardson-Walsh as Team GB's flag-bearer for the Olympic closing ceremony only added to the intensity of the coverage. It was a privilege that Richardson-Walsh accepted with typical humility.

'There are so many athletes here who have achieved great things in Rio and I'm incredibly surprised and excited to carry the flag,' said Kate ahead of the ceremony. 'I'm very aware of the magnitude of this honour having been part of this magnificent team who have just excelled in so many ways and in so many sports. I feel it's such a huge honour for me and for hockey as a sport.'

Team GB's Chef de Mission Mark England was in no doubt that she was the perfect candidate for the role of marshalling the most successful British team in Olympic history into Rio's Maracanã Stadium. 'There is no one more fitting than Kate to lead Team GB into the closing ceremony in what has been the greatest

Kate Richardson-Walsh was named Team GB's flag-bearer for the 2016 Olympic Games Closing Ceremony.
Julian Finney / Getty Images

Triathlon gold medallist Alistair Brownlee (bottom right) and gold medal-winning swimmer
Adam Peaty (top right) join the hockey party on the flight home.
Alex Livesey / Stringer / Getty Images

British sporting triumph of all time. For 16 years Kate has been on this journey with Team GB and has embodied the values and spirit of our Olympians throughout her career both as a captain and an athlete. The success of her and her team gripped the nation on Friday and no doubt inspired many to try to follow in her footsteps.'

If the intensity of the media coverage in the days following their gold medal success had come as a surprise, their reconnection with social media left many of the team astounded. 'A few of us have started signing back into our social media accounts now and we are finding that it has exploded,' said goalkeeper Maddie Hinch less that 24 hours after a final that had seen GB Hockey become the number one UK trend on Twitter. 'It has gone nuts! It has made us realise how much people have been watching us whilst we've been here.'

The decision of the players to disconnect from social media in order to focus solely on the task at hand had been a shrewd one, dramatically reducing the chances of being exposed to any external negativity in

the pressure-cooker environment of the Olympic Games. 'The last thing you need is some idiot tweeting to remind you that you'd had a bad match,' says Georgie Twigg, reflecting back on the reasoning behind the move. As it turned out, a seven-match winning run en route to the final meant that negativity would have been minimal. Twigg suggested that, in these circumstances, a connection to social media could have left the squad exposed to a very different issue: how to handle the huge weight of expectation from the British public. 'Thank goodness we didn't know from social media that nine million people were watching us play in the final. It massively helped us being away from it.'

As well as the many thousands of personal messages of congratulations, the team's sudden reconnection to social media allowed them to understand that the world outside of the hockey community had been stirred by what they had witnessed. Double Olympic gold medallist Dame Kelly Holmes took to Twitter to say that the hockey success was 'one of my best moments of the Games' before describing shootout heroine Maddie Hinch as a 'star', a point repeated by England football legend Gary Lineker and even referenced by Harry Potter author JK Rowling. Former England cricket captain Michael Vaughan went one better, informing the Twittersphere that he wanted Hinch 'as our new prime minister', while Sir Clive Woodward, the man who coached England to Rugby World Cup glory in 2003, described the gold medal success as a 'game changer for hockey'. London 2012 gold and Rio 2016 bronze long jump medallist Greg Rutherford stated that he believed that 'everyone will be inspired by GB Hockey'.

Rutherford's comments were soon backed up by facts as hockey clubs across the UK quickly reported a huge surge in interest, with thousands of new players eager to take up the sport and a host of others deciding to return to the game after years away. It was music to the ears of Sally Munday, chief operating officer of GB Hockey and England Hockey chief executive, who recognised the importance of the moment. Ahead of the squad's return to the UK, a plan was put in place to ensure that benefits to the sport would be long lasting. By

the end of the year, each individual athlete would have performed an average of over 70 public appearances per person across the United Kingdom, from school visits and club open days to talks to businesses and public engagements as well as satisfying interview, video and photoshoot requests that were now flooding in at unprecedented levels from the media. Upon their return home, Team GB's hockey stars would quickly realise that their lives would never be the same again.

At 10am on 23 August 2016, a British Airways Boeing 747 sporting a distinctive golden nose touched down at London's Heathrow Airport. Flight number BA2016, a plane renamed victoRIOus carrying a haul of 320 athletes and support staff, masses of sporting equipment and a record haul of gold, silver and bronze medals, had safely escorted Team GB back to British soil. During the 11-hour flight from Brazil the party had been in full swing, with Team GB's hockey girls at the centre of the celebration. Defensive duo Sam Quek and Laura Unsworth took the opportunity to dress up as British Airways cabin crew, being pictured ready, willing and able to serve champagne to their fellow athletes and delaying the serving of dinner by two hours. The

Sam Quek and Laura Unsworth take charge of the refreshments on British Airways flight number 2016 from Rio de Janeiro to London, with bewildered gymnastics double gold medallist Max Whitlock looking on.
Alex Livesey / Stringer / Getty Images

team were also at the heart of a fully committed rendition of 'God Save the Queen', with the footage filmed by Olympic 4x100m relay bronze medallist Asha Philip quickly going viral and featuring heavily on news channels before the team had even exited the plane.

Following a memorable photoshoot of dozens of Team GB medallists standing on the steps of the aircraft, the athletes headed to the arrivals hall at Terminal 5 where a mass of fans had gathered in wait to welcome their returning heroes. Amongst the fans were dozens of children – boys and girls – dressed in their club hockey kit, all waiting for the chance to meet their idols. It was a situation that left Helen Richardson-Walsh struggling to come to terms with what she was experiencing.

'Coming back to this is just incredible,' said an overwhelmed Richardson-Walsh, speaking to GB Hockey. 'I can't quite comprehend what is happening right now. When we set out on this journey a few years ago we created our vision. Be the difference, create history and inspire the future. And from what I am seeing it looks like we are inspiring the future and that's just fantastic for the game. I have just been told by some guy that he has gone down to his local club and it was full! They can't take any more players, it is just incredible!'

The mantra of inspiring the future and being role models to hockey's next generation was a common theme running through the many interviews that came in the immediate aftermath of the gold medal triumph. But what did it really mean? In an interview with Athens 2004 Olympic sprint relay gold medallist Darren Campbell for the BBC's *Get Inspired* show on Radio 5 Live, Sam Quek gave a very clear answer.

'That didn't just happen overnight, it wasn't a flippant decision that we were going to inspire the future,' said the defender, speaking to Campbell on a promotional visit to Bowdon Hockey Club, the club she joined as a 15-year-old before going on to represent it in the English National League. 'It was about how we are going to behave on the pitch when a small child is watching you, or a young girl, or an elder woman who might want to get involved in sport. When they are watching us on the pitch, what are they seeing? You see so many kids here who have just joined this club on the back of us winning gold. We want to inspire kids to get down to the clubs where they will make loads of new friends, become leaders and excel in so many more things. If we have done that, whether it is one, two or hundreds of thousands of kids then we have done our job because they are the future of our sport.'

As well as the influence on a new generation of players (GB Hockey revealed that player numbers increased by 10,000 in the months following the gold medal success, with almost as many boys taking up the

Team GB's athletes stand in front of the now iconic golden-nosed Boeing 747, a plane renamed 'victoRIOus' by British Airways especially for the occasion.
Stuart C. Wilson / Stringer / Getty Images

sport as girls), the team also found themselves being courted by the corporate world to speak at various business events, as Crista Cullen explains. 'Fundamentally, they want to know how you get a performance team to deliver when under pressure. We were able to do that purely on the basis that each individual was selected for having attributes that they had both in training and matches, and when under pressure, each individual took themselves away from the moment and was able to deliver. Collectively as a team we were able to gain momentum through the tournament thanks to our work ethic and team spirit, and that won people's hearts. I don't think we can ever lose sight of that.'

Cullen readily admits that the aftermath of the gold medal success was all rather surreal, as hockey players are not generally used to getting that level of attention. However, she was quick to point out that it was all a by-product of years of meticulous planning and preparation and was not an opportunity to be wasted.

'It all happened because a lot of people committed a lot of time in order to try to create an environment in which we could succeed,' continued Cullen, who became an Olympic gold medallist the day before her 31st birthday. 'It was important that we, the governing body and the individuals with the squad who were successful, took responsibility and tried to relish this moment. We wanted more people to be playing our sport, more people talking about hockey and more people aspiring to recreate what we were lucky enough to achieve.'

Nicola White shared a moving collection of letters that she had received from the Year 5 pupils of St Anne's School in Lydgate, which were written after the children were inspired by the exploits of the women's hockey team in Rio.
Nicola White

An observant spectator during the Rio 2016 Olympic Games may have spotted Danny Kerry taking a deep inhale and then very slowly letting the air back out in one long breath. 'It's the simplest and most effective way I know of keeping calm,' explains the Team GB women's hockey coach. 'A lot of people said I looked quite calm during the games but, if I'm honest, I can often take a catastrophic approach and see a loss way before we have actually lost a game. That is an element of my coaching I am working on.'

Since the gold medal in Rio de Janeiro, Danny Kerry has been hailed a master tactician and one of the best coaches in not just hockey, but team sports generally. Over the course of four months following Rio 2016, Kerry was named the BT Sports Coach of the Year, Team GB Coach of the Year and then, the biggest accolade of them all – the International Hockey Federation Coach of the Year. With a voting panel consisting of fellow international coaches, winning the FIH award in an Olympic year is a prize that Kerry treasures greatly.

Kerry's Olympic success prompted England Rugby head coach Eddie Jones to invite him to talk to his own international coaching team. In Kerry's own words: 'The guys at England Rugby basically plugged me in and downloaded me.'

But it has not always been that way. Kerry's megawatt smile when his team wins is legendary; but a gallery of images of Kerry over the past 11 years has far more pictures of the coach grimacing, clutching his head or simply scowling.

'I do find it difficult to hide my emotions,' Kerry admits and, in an effort to stop his annoyance and frustration filtering to the team, he has taken to watching matches from a position high in the stands. The fun for the camera teams at a hockey tournament is to be found in swinging the lens around the stand trying to find the coach when his team makes a mistake. Even with the trademark cap pulled over his head to hide his expression, Kerry slumped low in his seat or slapping his clipboard, is still unable to disguise his body language.

However, in recent years, one of the most admirable things about the Olympic gold medal-winning coach has been his ability and willingness to keep learning and improving upon his own performance. For most coaches, the aim is to keep developing the players: for Kerry, that cannot happen unless he continues pushing his own coaching to new levels as well.

'He has changed a hell of a lot,' is Georgie Twigg's assessment of Kerry. Twigg first came into the senior international set-up in 2010 and, during that time, she says the coach has 'embraced fluidity' and allowed an element of 'challenge and control' to pass to the players.

'He has always been the most fantastic tactician, he knows the game inside out,' she says, 'but he now lets others take control. For instance, allowing Craig Keegan to work with the forwards, all of whom have so much flair. For me, the big difference between Rio 2016 and London 2012 was our forwards. When we were on the attack in Rio we looked likely to score.

'When you look at how many goalscoring chances we had in the Olympic final compared to Holland, it wasn't many but we scored them. There is a clear difference in the way that our coaches have been allowed to work with the forwards which has allowed that to happen.'

Kerry himself is quick to admit that he has been through some tough times in his development as a coach. The Beijing 2008 Olympic Games was a seminal moment, and he says that he was on the verge of stepping away from the role all together. On the surface, he had done no wrong. The team went to Beijing ranked 11th in the world and they finished sixth, which was no mean feat. But, for Kerry and his charges, things

Danny Kerry.
Koen Suyk

were far from perfect. In fact, for the coach, it was one of the most challenging times of his coaching career.

Kerry had taken over as head coach to the Great Britain side in 2005, at a difficult time in the team's history. Under head coach Tricia Heberle, they had spectacularly failed to qualify for the Athens 2004 Olympic Games and the next few years were to prove difficult for both players and coaches as the squad sought to rebuild its confidence and world standing. A sixth-place finish at the Beijing 2008 Olympic Games was an improvement on what had gone before, but it was clear that there was a huge amount of work still to do.

Kerry shoulders a lot of responsibility for the failure to perform in Beijing, and after confronting his demons – both real and imagined – he made a pledge to change the way he coached and interacted with his players.

Looking back, Kerry is honest when he talks about his own personal development. 'Up to and during the Beijing Olympics I had this mindset that I couldn't let my emotions show. I had to internalise

everything and that eventually led to a difficult relationship with some of my players.'

And so, Kerry set about changing things. He had always been a man who thought deeply about the coaching process, now he had to apply those levels of reflection to his own performance.

'I thought I had given everything for the team,' says Kerry in an interview published on the website Sports Coach UK. 'But in the review process, the athlete group and the staff I worked with really tore me to pieces. They pretty much called me "grumpy, miserable and unapproachable". I felt betrayed.

'There was a lot of soul-searching at the time. The feedback was pretty harrowing.'

A dejected Kerry returned home and he admits that it was largely the support of his wife, Lisa, that persuaded him that he was the person for the role.

'Lisa told me I was not the person that people thought I was but I admit, I came very close to walking away. For people to turn round who you have really respected to effectively character assassinate you was really tough. But actually, they were right.

Coach and captain. Danny Kerry and Kate Richardson-Walsh developed a special partnership over nearly a decade.
Koen Suyk

'My way of working was to try to defeat the world by knowledge, and I was very much stuck in my laptop, looking at videos, understanding the performance and planning for the next one. I literally wasn't stepping outside my room in the Olympic village to talk to people and engage them in conversations, which sometimes gets to the heart of what performance is all about. I was very much about tactical execution and the knowledge of hockey rather than the knowledge of human beings.'

One of the players who has been part of Kerry's squad from day one is defender and drag-flick specialist Crista Cullen, who agrees that Beijing was the catalyst for the emergence of a new-look head coach and a different culture within the squad.

'One of the biggest lessons Danny learnt from the Beijing experience was that each player is an individual and to get the best from his squad, he needed to know what made each person tick.

'He has gone through a lot of changes both as a coach and as a person since 2005,' she says. 'Coaching a women's international side has its complications and it took him a little while to figure out how best to do that.

'Beijing was difficult for him and for the players but full credit to the national governing body because they stuck by him. Over time, he has used every bit of experience, good or bad, to learn how to work with athletes and that has led to a very different style of coaching and a very different style of player.'

Cullen says that the lack of success in Beijing and fragmentation among groups of players really was at the heart of the problem facing Kerry and England Hockey. But, she adds, that all changed when London won the right to host the 2012 Olympic Games.

'We had funding to enable us to run a centralised programme, which allowed more contact time. There were more players on the central programme, allowing Danny and his staff to build a new culture and address the negative stuff that had happened in Beijing. We all set about creating a better culture, which meant a more nurturing, supportive and caring environment.'

Running alongside the changes to the group culture was a change in approach from the head coach. Players and the other staff are united as they talk

Strong leadership provided by Kerry and Richardson-Walsh was core to Team GB's success.
Frank Uijlenbroek

All smiles: Kerry and Susannah Townsend enjoy a moment during Rio 2016.

Frank Uijlenbroek

about Danny's obsession with detail and his need to control every aspect of the game. However, with a steely determination and no little angst, Kerry started to loosen his grip and the new approach began to pay dividends thanks to the players' growing trust in their coach and his vision for the future.

As Beijing receded and London loomed close, Kerry's outward demeanour became lighter, less introvert: even the vocabulary changed. From talking about the coach 'owning the performance', it was now all about collective ownership, distributed leadership and common purpose.

'I do live inside my head a lot, even now,' says Kerry. 'If I am inside my own head, thinking, especially around the athlete group, that can appear as if I am unapproachable. I'm not. My face might look like I'm in a mood, and athletes under pressure can potentially read into that.

'I've made a conscious effort for the athletes to try to smile, have fun and show them I do enjoy it. I just did a lot of thinking about how I had worked, and how I could work better. I did do a lot of reading, but probably more importantly I was willing to adapt and evolve how I coached.'

Twigg agrees with Kerry's self-assessment: 'I think Danny has worked hard on enhancing his relationship with the group and has worked with Andrea (Furst), our psychologist, to make sure that he can be the best version of himself. Everyone has negative traits, I think Danny knows what his are and works hard on those as he wants the best for everyone else. I've definitely seen a change (over the past seven years) in that respect.'

The result of this period of self-reflection and adaptation has been astonishing. Kerry has managed to transform himself from a coach who could be remote, and often difficult to communicate with, to a coach who is not afraid to let his emotions show. Famously, Kerry broke down in tears on television when he announced the squad for London 2012. It was a moment that both astonished and touched many of his squad.

The new, communicative and emotional coach now has a much more harmonious relationship with his players. Speaking before Rio 2016, captain Kate Richardson-Walsh said: 'There has been a lot of change since 2008. Danny will always spend a lot of time thinking how can everything be better and that includes himself. How he coaches a training session, how he plans the session, how this is communicated with players and how he can best leverage on the strengths of the group.'

Crista Cullen also reflects back: 'I think Danny has learned a lot about himself and how he has to best treat and work with athletes, culminating in a very different style of coaching. It was less prescribed and more

fundamental learning, learning as a group and also about each other, because ultimately we are the ones who have to deliver on a performance platform.

'By the time we got to Rio, it was a less authoritarian style, not being told what to do, where to do it and how to do it and therefore we were less mechanical in our approach to deliver. It allowed us to play a little bit more through the intelligence of the players, who were able to read the situations and understand the balance between risk and opportunity and being empowered to make that decision as athletes.' But, she adds: 'I think it took him three cycles to get there.

'Now, what Danny – and it's not just Danny but the whole coaching team – have created is something special, a culture of trust and buy-in.'

While Danny Kerry's change in behaviour and relationship with his players has been a talking point, what has also emerged is the detailed planning that the coach and his staff poured into their preparations for Rio 2016. Always a deep thinker, now it seemed that Kerry was spending all his waking moments planning for every eventuality. As Crista Cullen points out, 'There is always an element of luck in sport,' but Kerry and his team were determined to reduce the impact of chance and luck as much as was humanly possible.

Kerry's second reign had started well. A silver medal with England at the 2014 Commonwealth Games came just three months after the debacle of the World Cup. It marked one small step along the road to recovery for the English members of the Great Britain squad, but it was also another timely piece of silverware. A trawl through the medals that England and Great Britain has won under Kerry's stewardship shows that when it really, really matters, Kerry's teams usually deliver.

It is a point with which Karen Brown, assistant coach to Kerry for eight years, makes strongly. 'People talk about our ups and downs but really that is not a fair reflection. We did have a blip at the World Cup, but I think that everyone forgets that since Beijing we have been consistently winning medals. We had been building for the moment in Rio for eight years. Our preparations didn't begin with a few weeks to go, they had been thought through and tested time and again.'

While the ability to reinvent himself as a coach has won Kerry plaudits, it is his practical session planning that has made other coaches sit up and take note. One of the key things about the team at Rio 2016 was their ability to make logical decisions under enormous pressure. It is not something that has happened by accident, as Kerry explains: 'During training, we create situations that the players may face in the game itself

Kerry addresses his troops.

Frank Uijlenbroek

and then we pile the pressure on so that the players get used to making decisions in tough circumstances.

'The "posh" word for it is to create multiple "affordances" to practice the situation you want. What this means is that the more times you put the player in a situation, you create greater capacity for the athlete to problem solve that situation in real time.'

In other words, much of the Great Britain hockey team's training time is spent working on games-based play. This is at the other end of the spectrum from the isolated technical practices that so many coaches insist on putting their teams and players through. 'We don't use isolated drills because they are simply not relevant to the game situation,' says Kerry. 'So many coaches, in all sports, use isolated skills in their coaching because it is what they experienced themselves as players.'

It is not a new idea. Rod Thorpe, a former lecturer at Loughborough University, developed his Teaching Games for Understanding theory back in the 1980s after witnessing games-based learning among school children in New Zealand. The premise was simple: the best way to learn how to read the game and make good decisions was to play the game and develop an ability to read the cues offered by the outside environment.

Kerry, a former student of Thorpe's at Loughborough, believes it is the best way of coaching a team sport. 'Team sports create chaotic and contextually random situations. That is what we try to both mirror and really amplify. For example, a sample session might include the instruction, "you can only pass forwards" or "you must keep the ball in the left-hand channel", it is about creating an overly chaotic environment so it becomes second nature to work within it and make decisions.'

Was this how Team GB managed to overcome a team that spent much of the match putting them under pressure? 'The Dutch were certainly on top for much of the first half (of the Rio 2016 Olympic final). We had to soak up the pressure but that is what I am talking about; we didn't crack under the pressure because, as a squad, we have been putting ourselves under that sort of pressure every time we train.

'We know for example that globally, and particularly in the case of Australia and Netherlands, the teams play with a high zonal press. We train to cope with that and to recognise the cues that might affect our decision-making.'

Kerry's theory is simple. He wants to give the players a broader and better base of decision-making capacity under pressure. The advantage of this approach was outlined by goalkeeper Maddie Hinch when she explained how she so regularly gets the better

Danny Kerry, presenting flowers to future Olympic gold medallist Laura Unsworth on the occasion of her 100th international appearance, in the England versus Scotland match at the EuroHockey Nations Championships 2013 in Boom, Belgium.
Frank Uijlenbroek

of her opponents when matches go to shootouts. 'I watch video after video of the attacking players in these scenarios. I know that under pressure a player will revert to type. If they usually go to the right, in the pressured situation of an Olympic final they are likely to go right. If I use my movements to increase the pressure on them, then I can be even more certain of how they will react.'

Just as Hinch's goalkeeping notebook became the stuff of legends following the gold medal win, so 'Thinking Thursday' has become part of hockey's common parlance. This was the day that Kerry earmarked for putting his players under extreme pressure. Based on military principles, the idea is to put the players under enormous physical and mental stress and then challenge them to solve problems. Exhausted, stressed and pressured, the players still had to make the right decision. Now, with gold medals hanging around their necks, the players joke about it, but it is one of many reasons they are now wearing those medals.

Since Rio 2016, the players have come forward to pay tribute to their coach. Alex Danson has called him 'the best tactical coach in the world', while Kate Richardson-Walsh says: 'Danny is a master tactician. He understands the game and spends hours looking at the opposition to find the little differences we can make in our games, the little tweaks we can make tactically game to game. I think that's partly won us this medal.

'The other thing Danny is really strong on is team culture. When he came in a couple of years ago (after Jason Lee's departure), he really worked hard with the leadership group – myself, Helen (Richardson-Walsh) and Alex (Danson), Emily Maguire and Ashleigh Ball – to really form the culture of this squad.

'I think that's what you see,' she adds. 'When you see us running out together, when you see us huddling at the end of a game, running off to the changing room at half-time, that's culture. That's what makes us tick, that's what makes us strong, that's what makes us tight. So under pressure small cracks don't become big ones. We can deal with all those stresses and pressures together as a unit.'

Three significant moments in the past two seasons indicate just how far Kerry has come with his team.

In the Champions Trophy in London, a matter of weeks before the Rio 2016 Olympic Games, Kerry asked his team to do something that is anathema to most players. In the pool match against the USA, he asked them not to play their 'A' game. The result was a loss in front of a passionate, and disappointed home crowd.

After the game, Lily Owsley said: 'The first thing to say is we're focusing on sticking together as a team. We believe this has no reflection on how we will do at Rio. It's important to keep believing and keep doing what we do and it'll come together at the right time.'

Owsley's assertion that this was no reflection on how they would play at Rio 2016 was no word of a lie. Instead, Team GB did bring their 'A' game to their pool match against the USA and claimed a hugely significant victory. 'There was no way I wanted Craig Parnham (USA coach) to see how we would play in Rio. It was difficult for the team, but with gold medals around their necks, who is smiling now?' said Kerry.

The second significant moment came when the squad came together just weeks before the Olympic Games to decide upon their social media strategy. Had social media been such a huge thing in Beijing 2008, there is no doubt that the coach would have imposed a ban throughout the tournament. Not Kerry, the 2016 version. 'It was tough,' says Kerry with a grin. 'Every part of my brain was screaming to say "no social media", but I knew it had to come from the team.'

In fact, the debate twisted and turned for days, much to the coach's quiet agony, but in the end a team decision to ban all social media was agreed and Kerry breathed easily. 'It couldn't come from me or the coaching staff,' he explains. 'This was something that they had to decide and everyone had to buy into a collective decision.'

'It seems such a little thing now,' reflects Georgie Twigg, 'but actually it was incredibly powerful. We discussed and covered all sorts of angles, there were some very deep discussions. Some people just said

they were not affected by social media but, in fact, if you have a bad game and then just keep reading comments about it, that can destroy your confidence. We made the decision as a group and it worked. It kept us in a bubble and we really had no idea of the impact we were having back home.'

The final moment that proved that Kerry's belief in players taking responsibility for their actions was probably the most telling and certainly had the most memorable outcome.

The day before the final, the team were at the practice pitch. On the adjacent pitch the Netherlands were training. Eventually it was time to practice shootouts in preparation for a draw in the final. Everyone who might be called upon was taking the opportunity to get one last practice in. It came to Hollie Webb's turn.

'No,' she said. 'I've practised this time and again, I am not going to give anything away to the Dutch.'

'One last chance to practice,' was the collective exhortation from her team. Webb was adamant. Logic told her that one more practice wasn't going to change her ability to score but it might give away vital information to tomorrow's opponents.

'It is the ability to think for themselves and make logical decisions that will turn players from good players into winning players,' says Kerry. The proof of his wisdom lies in Webb's face as she turned and faced her team-mates after scoring the goal that won gold.

Year	Team	Tournament	Position Achieved
2005	England	KT Cup, Seoul (KOR)	Gold Medal
	England	EuroHockey Nations Championship, Dublin (IRL)	Bronze Medal
2006	England	Hockey World Cup Qualifier, Rome (ITA)	Gold Medal
	England	Commonwealth Games, Melbourne (AUS)	Bronze Medal
2007	England	EuroHockey Nations Championship, Manchester (ENG)	Bronze & direct Olympic qualification for Team GB
2008	Team GB	Beijing 2008 Olympic Games (CHN)	6th
2009	England	EuroHockey Nations Championship, Amsterdam (NED)	Bronze
2010	England	Hockey Champions Trophy, Nottingham (ENG)	Bronze
	England	Hockey World Cup, Rosario (ARG)	Bronze
	England	Commonwealth Games, New Delhi (IND)	Bronze
2011	England	EuroHockey Nations Championship, Mönchengladbach (GER)	Bronze
2012	Great Britain	Hockey Champions Trophy, Rosario (ARG)	Silver
	Team GB	London 2012 Olympic Games (GBR)	Bronze
2014	England	2014 Commonwealth Games, Glasgow (SCO)	Silver
2015	Team GB	Hockey World League Semi-Final (Olympic Qualification Tournament), Valencia (ESP)	Winners
	England	EuroHockey Nations Championship, London (ENG)	Gold
2016	Team GB	Rio 2016 Olympic Games (BRA)	Gold

Chapter 12

Planning to Win

'It wasn't like we were out jogging in Rio one day and just stumbled over a gold medal,' says Craig Keegan as he reflects upon the four years that led from a bronze at London 2012 to gold at Rio 2016.

The emerging picture from the Rio 2016 narrative is one of meticulous planning in which every last detail was considered from every angle. While Danny Kerry is undoubtedly the mastermind behind the whole plan, in order to prepare the squad to the degree he deemed necessary to return with gold, it was essential that there was a wealth of support from the people surrounding him.

Two of the most important people in this process were the assistant coaches, Karen Brown and Craig Keegan, both highly experienced coaches, both stubborn individuals, but both of whom believed in the team culture and belief that Kerry was building.

That culture included talking about every eventuality, planning every minute detail, sharing the leadership responsibilities and ensuring that every single person knew exactly what their role was at any given time.

'From the time we arrived two weeks before the Games started, it was just about the players getting to the village and finding their way around,' says Karen Brown as she explains just how the meticulous planning was implemented. 'We always trained at the venue, so it was about finding the quickest, most reliable routes and trying to anticipate any problems we might encounter on the journey. Those were busy days, as we just tried to get into matchday routines as quickly as possible.'

The intricate planning and microscopic attention to detail were a challenge as they required everyone to follow instructions, but it was accepted because everyone could see the rationale behind such planning. Take for instance, the insistence by the coaching team that the players did not return to their rooms between meals and meetings. 'The players' rooms were on the ninth floor of the hotel,' says Brown. 'The dining room was 1,000 steps away, and the meeting rooms were close by. If the players went back to their rooms they expended another 1,000 steps – that matters when it comes to matchday.'

While planning for all eventualities was onerous but achievable, a tougher challenge was instilling a culture that everyone bought into – athletes and staff. Both Keegan and Brown acknowledge that this was a much longer process and one that is still ongoing.

For goalkeeping coach John Hurst, a veteran of many Olympic campaigns as both a player, a coach and a manager, building a team culture among the staff was a vital part of the whole jigsaw. 'Performance sport exists on a knife edge, particularly so as a major event

Craig Keegan, whose work with Great Britain's attacking players has been widely praised by the athletes.
Koen Suyk

A legendary player in her own right, Karen Brown commanded the respect of all when it came to discussions about defensive tactics.
Frank Uijlenbroek

approaches,' said Hurst, a man regularly name-checked by England and Great Britain's finest goalkeepers, including Maddie Hinch, as pivotal to their development on the international stage. 'It doesn't take much of a wobble to bring the whole thing crashing down, so creating bonds between the group of athletes, the group of staff and between athletes and staff is a vital part of the whole. I believe there were several important moments within the staff group that led to us being very close by the time we reached Rio.

'We had several staff changes over the cycle. Jason Lee was replaced as head coach in 2014, leading to Danny taking over and the subsequent appointment of Andrea Furst as psychologist. Amber Luzar replaced Maggie Souyave as analyst after the Commonwealth Games and, potentially, so many changes might have caused a negative effect on the squad. It didn't and I think this was down to us all trying very hard to make it work, as well as some important initiatives instigated by Andrea, which really made a difference.'

Hurst points to some moments of 'deep soul searching by the staff', where they were all encouraged to discuss what they behaved like in different scenarios. 'The title was "Good Day, Bad Day", explains Hurst. 'Essentially, it involved us explaining to the staff group what we were like when having a good day and a bad day and what others could do to help us on a bad day. This led to the rest of the group asking very deep questions and saying what we thought about each individual's behaviour. It was emotional, it was hard-hitting and we all emerged from it knowing what others thought about us and with a plan to help ourselves and each other.'

The most hard-hitting of these sessions took place on the Australia tour in February 2016. Hurst says of that time, 'It really aided our working relationship, our unity and our friendship. I really think that we would have done anything for each other and this was demonstrated in Valencia at the Olympic Qualifier in 2015 when I had a health issue. I collapsed just before the tournament which could have had a negative effect on staff and athletes. It seemed to have the reverse. My colleagues were quite superb in their handling of the entire incident from initial help when it happened to support for me through it. The athletes, too, were brilliant and I felt they wanted to "win for Hursty".'

Hurst took a tumble, albeit just a minor trip, again in Rio, causing Georgie Twigg to quip, 'He's fallen over again, we will win now….'.

For Keegan, his second role within England Hockey as U21 coach was part of the process to ensure the culture created was sustained as players and staff left and joined the programme. For Brown, it was a process that had started straight after Beijing 2008, when she had joined the programme as assistant coach. And the fruits were only just beginning to yield.

This was the culture that saw the team self-impose a social media ban throughout both the London 2012 and Rio 2016 Olympic Games; it was the culture that saw Keegan himself miss the Opening Ceremony in Brazil because he wanted to take one more look at his notes on how Australia (the team's opponents the next day) played; it was the culture that meant while Dutch coach Alyson Annan was marching from player to player and raising their levels of adrenaline prior to the nerve-wracking shootout for Olympic gold, Kerry was quietly telling his players that this was no different to a day at Bisham Abbey.

The coaching triumvirate of Kerry, Brown and Keegan, backed up by Hurst, Furst and Luzar, worked ceaselessly to create the culture they wanted, working on the language used around the group, the non-verbal communication, the leadership group, the sharing of responsibilities. No area of the players' lives was left unexamined for ways that the prevailing culture could be reinforced. For Keegan, this level of teamwork was an eye-opener.

'Some teams talk about an underlying culture, and some teams do portray that from time to time, but we believed it and lived it. We genuinely did. It was eye-opening for me because I had always worked on team dynamics and a tight team culture but they had never quite come together as the Rio squad did. It was the environment as well, we were so closely knit and we were training together so often that it gave us the ability to grow the culture we did.'

Craig Keegan joined the Great Britain senior programme in 2013. Born in Tasmania, Australia, he moved to England when he was 26 to take up a role as player/coach to Premier League side Beeston, where he quickly demonstrated his goalscoring credentials. In 2008, Keegan joined England Hockey as head coach of the National Performance Centre in Loughborough,

Karen Brown and Craig Keegan immediately following Team GB's semi-final victory over New Zealand at Rio 2016.
Frank Uijlenbroek

during which time he coached both the men's and women's national age group squads. He was also head coach to the women's U21 side, leading them to two Junior World Cups and, more importantly for the long term, developing the same culture within the next generation of players.

The coach, who is now director of performance sport at Derby University, explains his role within the Great Britain and England set-up: 'I was called assistant coach but, if we were in America, I would be the "offensive coach", while Karen (Brown) would be the "defensive coach". I like that terminology because it simplifies the areas we were looking after. I was tasked with the job of improving our ability to score goals and taking our approach away from "goal shooting" sessions to "goal scoring" sessions. That was one of the strap-lines or terminologies I changed so the players understood that the session was about goal scoring, not shooting.'

Changing terminology was one of the ways that Kerry and his team were also changing attitudes and

The Team GB huddle ahead of the medal ceremony in Rio, with goalkeeping coach John Hurst smiling in the centre.
Frank Uijlenbroek

it was something in which Keegan whole-heartedly believed: 'Goal scoring is an attitude. Yes, you need basic skill and technical ability to be able to execute the skill of shooting, but it's the attitude that scores the goal.'

Putting the ball into the net was one of the areas that the coaches had highlighted as a weakness among the Team GB squad going into the Rio 2016 cycle. 'Statistically, we just didn't shoot enough,' says Keegan, adding: 'It is a cultural thing and not something that can be changed across the board overnight.' But, the Australian knew it was something he could change within the squad of players.

'It is why someone like Alex (Danson) will always score, because she has that single-minded attitude "I'm going to score" and that is what sets people such as her apart. We have better technicians in the team than Alex but her attitude towards goalscoring is amazing.'

Like Kerry, Keegan was concerned about giving his players the knowledge and experience to make good decisions in tricky situations. 'A deep part of my philosophy as a coach is to create an environment for people to excel in,' he says, echoing Kerry's support for games-based learning. 'The skill of a coach is to set up the skill and the environment for players to think their way through.

'I am a strong believer in that but I also believe there is a need for some deep-reaching, highly skilled sessions to sit within those more game-based, constraints-led sessions. I was always pushing for those technical sessions where we could practise a skill unopposed in a "grooving and moulding" type of approach.'

This is a minor deviation from Kerry's coaching philosophy but, says Keegan, a situation in which all the coaches think identically would never work. 'Some challenge is healthy and we were certainly never made to feel that we couldn't put across our view.'

Nowhere was this open attitude more evident than in the selection process; something that Keegan looks back on with real admiration: 'The selection process was so thorough, we really covered every base possible. Within the coaching group we had different views but there were no barriers up to discussing our views.

'There was never a "no, I don't agree with you" approach, it was always about looking at every option. But the three of us didn't always agree when we went into the process. Karen and Danny had worked together for a number of years before I came in and my viewpoint was very different to theirs in many ways. I think that helped freshen up the approach.

'I really enjoyed the selection approach, some of those meetings were fascinating. It was a real insight into personalities and character and I learnt a huge amount.'

The tricky moments came as the final few names went onto the selection sheet. While Karen Brown and Craig were firmly in one camp, Danny Kerry had a different name he wanted to add to the list. Kerry himself says he spent an entire night mulling it over before he decided to go with Keegan and Brown's choice.

It was a decision that astonished both his assistants. 'It certainly surprised both of us,' says Keegan. 'He had made it very clear that as head coach he would have the final say and we thought that was right. But thankfully, once we had made that decision he was 100 per cent on board. Once the decision was made then "bang" we were on the job, this was the group that was going to do it.'

Rio 2016 was Keegan's first Olympic Games, but for his defensive counterpart Karen Brown this was a fifth Games – three times as a player (Seoul 1988; Barcelona 1992, where the team won bronze; and Atlanta 1996) and two as a coach (London 2012 and Rio 2016) – but when the final whistle went, she felt strangely underwhelmed.

'It was weird,' she says. 'You've done the job you have been preparing for and then you are sitting on the team bench watching it all unravel in front of you. It's very different to when you are watching on television, then it is emotional and you feel an outpouring because you are so emotionally involved for intense periods of time. We had been living for and preparing for this moment for months. It was a job well done.

'We had been building towards this for the last eight years. We used everything we had learnt during past experiences to decide what worked and what didn't work. That sounds simple but it is actually very difficult.'

While the three coaches were focussed on the techniques, tactics and psychology of the game, another vital aspect of the win was the incredible athleticism and fitness of the players. Kerry had said prior to the Olympic Games that he wanted to take athletes who could get through eight games in two weeks. There was no room in this squad for fragility. Widely credited with getting the players to where they needed to be in terms of fitness was the strength and conditioning coach Ben Rosenblatt, who joined the coaching staff in October 2013.

'It was really clear to me from the start that there was a high degree of physical fitness among the players, but Jason Lee (coach in 2013) wanted the fitness to reflect the core skills the players needed for their individual game,' says Rosenblatt.

'There was also a requirement to make the players more durable, so they can endure the tough training that would help them develop tactically and skill-wise.'

This translated into enabling the players to firstly, withstand high levels of intense physical training, and second, to develop tournament durability – the ability to

Strength and conditioning coach Ben Rosenblatt and team psychologist Andrea Furst watch on from the stands.
Koen Suyk

keep performing for the seven or eight games of a high level of competition such as the Olympic Games.

'I think Townno (Susannah Townsend) is probably the best example of our approach,' says Rosenblatt. 'She is a great player going forwards but, two years out from Rio 2016, she wasn't a great player going backwards. We needed to make her track back hard and become as effective going backwards as she was going forwards.'

Rosenblatt explains that he was tasked with finding a physical solution to Townsend's weakness. 'Training was set up to look at the movements needed to track back. What did she need to do? What movements and muscles were involved? Then we would put her in a training situation where she was forced to do only those movements needed to track backwards.'

Townsend's training focus was just one example. Rosenblatt and his team of strength and conditioning coaches soon had the whole squad working on elements of their fitness pertinent to their roles and responsibilities on the pitch. 'They were physically very

capable, we had to make the fitness elements link to the movements they would do in a match.'

In the early days, this brought problems. The players were used to working very hard and seeing immediate change. Under the traditional school of thought, if you were working on your sprinting, you should get faster. In fact, says Rosenblatt, that wasn't always the case. 'The first time the players realised what we were aiming for was the moment when they were on the pitch and they won the ball more frequently or they had more success when tracking back. They had to learn to measure performance on the pitch, not in pure objective measures. The race was between the player and her opponent rather than anything measurable in the gym.'

But, change of this magnitude takes time and a year into Rosenblatt's appointment the results were not showing. 'At the World Cup (2014) there is no doubt about it, we got out-run,' says Rosenblatt with his usual honesty.

'Change always meets resistance. We had to really set about establishing behaviours but I also wanted the players to say what those behaviours should be. We had a lot of one-to-one meetings, lots of small group meetings and then some whole group stuff. Eventually, we all came to one viewpoint.

'The group then were quite passive and dependent. They wanted me to tell them what to do, and if it didn't work, then that was my responsibility. I wanted to change that mindset so they could make effective decisions about their own fitness. The players should be able to talk to the skills coach and say "what is it that I need to do in order to get better?" That is something they started to do and it is really what I hope they are building on now.'

While Brown, Keegan and Rosenblatt had definite roles within the squad, improving skills, tactics and fitness, one person, who has been name checked time and again as key to the whole process is sports psychologist Andrea Furst.

She explains that her role was to make sure that, not only were the players in the best frame of mind to perform, but that the coaches were too. 'Too many times I have seen the best prepared teams come undone because the staff took their eye off the ball,' is a favourite refrain of Kerry's. And the head coach was determined that would not happen in Rio.

'I worked with Danny to identify the mindset in which he performed his best during games,' says Furst – an Australian who has worked with England Hockey and the Great Britain squad since 2013.

'This work was very similar to the way I work with athletes to become consistent at creating the "performance mindset" they want to have in order to perform on the pitch. Coaching is inevitably frustrating at times so we also worked on strategies to deal with the frustrations that arose during the games, specifically so that the communication from Danny to Keegs (Craig Keegan) and Karen, (Brown) who were on the bench, was as effective as possible.

'One of his key strengths is his tactical mind so the key aim was for him to be able to play this role consistently for the team during games. I went through the same process with Keegs and Karen as well – we treated everyone as performers.'

With the mental health of the athletes as important to performance as their physical health, Furst's presence was essential in the intense months leading up to Rio. 'There is a great deal of pressure and expectation on athletes and coaches in the elite sporting environment,' she says. 'Athletes are measured and monitored to within an inch of their lives inside these sporting organisations and teams. That is in addition to the attention they receive from

Susannah Townsend benefitted greatly from an athlete-specific fitness regime, according to strength and conditioning coach Ben Rosenblatt.
Frank Uijlenbroek

the outside general public through social media. There is not much of their life that is private.

'My role is to help athletes to understand themselves so they can perform consistently under the pressure of the highest level competition and also have respect for their brain and their mental health. So I want to create athletes who are confident and resilient

competitors as well as people who understand the demands that these environments place upon them and give them the space and skills to deal with the environment.'

Months on and in a different role, Karen Brown has had time to reflect upon those years of preparation. 'Looking back now, I am really proud of what we achieved, how we worked as a staff. We all had each others' back and everyone played their role.' She pauses and corrects herself: 'Everyone was allowed to do their role, that is what makes a successful team.'

Chapter 13

Target Tokyo 2020

Two days after the final of the women's hockey competition at the Rio 2016 Olympic Games, Team GB head coach Danny Kerry received a phone call from Sally Munday, GB Hockey's chief operating officer and chief executive of England Hockey, who was now back on British soil after witnessing the team's history-making exploits in Brazil. It was a call that she would not quickly forget.

'I phoned him to see how he was,' remembers Munday. 'I had just arrived back in the UK and it was Sunday evening in Rio, where he was still with the team. I asked him if he was basking in the glory of what he had achieved. His response was to tell me that he had actually spent the entire afternoon sitting in his room mind-mapping how Team GB was going to win gold in Tokyo (2020 Olympic Games). My jaw nearly hit the table. I said "for God's sake Danny, just enjoy the moment!"

'To be honest, I think it is a sign of the man that he is,' continues Munday. 'Plenty of others would have been out there milking it, snapping up lucrative speaking contracts or taking financially attractive coaching offers from all over the world. He was in real demand, as you'd expect an Olympic gold medal-winning coach to be, but he hasn't got a big ego. He is extremely loyal, not just to England and GB Hockey, but especially to this group of players, the ones who did not retire after Rio like Sophie Bray, Hollie Webb and Maddie Hinch. He simply wants his players to get more medals around their necks.'

Kerry's desire to prepare a masterplan in order to mount a successful title defence at Tokyo 2020 was an understandable viewpoint from a man who clearly had unfinished business with the team. However, to do it just 48 hours after the most remarkable success of his career may seem strange to some. So why did Kerry decide to draw what he described as 'the world's biggest mind-map' on Sunday 21 August 2016?

'I think that was just me decompressing and assimilating it all (the gold medal win),' says Kerry on reflection. 'It was just a case of getting it all out of my system, it was like talking therapy. I was just trying to get my head straight. A lot of that was asking myself questions such as, why did we win? What do we want to keep? What are we going to lose? What are the big risks? It just started from there.'

Over five hours, Danny Kerry scrutinised every element in meticulous detail. Ideas about changes to the athlete leadership and coaching staff models came to the fore, as well as a determination to embed a new culture into the group of athletes that he would be working with for the next four years. While many of the gold medallists from the Rio cycle would remain in the GB programme, Kerry recognised that one of the biggest challenges of the rebuilding process would be how the group would cope with the loss of experienced personnel both on and off the field. Also, for those Olympic gold medallists who had decided to commit to the programme for another four years, what would be their motivation?

'I think the challenge of success is as big as the challenge of failure, sometimes,' says Kerry, before looking at the drive for a gold medal at Tokyo 2020 from a metaphorical perspective. 'Why would you want to go to the moon? Well it's very aspirational to get there, but if you have already been, why would you want to go again? Some people, like myself, have a chronic need for achievement. You want to know you can do it. Others are looking for a different challenge in their life. My challenge is to give people enough time to make up their minds and try to understand themselves. But at the same time, the opposition are up and running and they are trying to find their own way to the moon. Their motivation remains, but a lot of our players have done it. It is my responsibility to be clear with my expectations. It is my job, and that of the national governing body, to do it again.'

In January 2017, Kerry revealed the 33 athletes that would be part of Great Britain's initial central programme building towards Tokyo 2020. Of the 18 athletes from the Rio cycle who had committed to the new programme, 12 had travelled to Brazil with the squad: Giselle Ansley, Sophie Bray, Alex Danson, Maddie Hinch, Shona McCallin, Lily Owsley, Susannah Townsend, Laura Unsworth, Hollie Webb and Nicola White as well as reserve athletes Joie Leigh and Ellie Watton. The Rio survivors were joined by a significant injection of new blood, with 15 athletes representing England, Scotland and Wales entering the central programme for the first time. The group was revealed after months of continuous assessment, with Kerry stating his firm belief that his new training group had all of the attributes that he was looking for.

'We have, I feel, a good depth of skilful, committed, smart, and athletic athletes who are eager to learn, develop and build on the legacy and momentum of the Rio Olympic cycle,' says Kerry. 'We have also retained an excellent core from the previous cycle, who no doubt will play a key role in passing on the values and behaviours that drive performance whilst evolving the culture for the coming cycle. With a home World Cup for England on the Queen Elizabeth Olympic Park in 2018, and the prospect of Team GB defending an Olympic title in Tokyo 2020, the challenges of this cycle are as clear, significant and exciting as ever. I believe this new squad has what it takes to shine again and continue to inspire future generations to play our sport.'

Sophie Bray (this picture), Hollie Webb (p178) and Maddie Hinch (p179) are likely to be key figures in the Great Britain set-up for many years to come.
Frank Uijlenbroek

One of the most senior members of the new-look Great Britain training squad is star striker Alex Danson, a player who made her first senior international appearance way back in 2001 at the tender age of 16. After becoming an Olympic gold medallist in 2016, some 15 years after debuting against Germany, it was hardly surprising that questions surrounding her ongoing involvement were rife.

'There were a lot of people who wondered why I would want to continue, having achieved something I had dreamed of doing since I was a kid,' says Danson, who had an extended break before rejoining the training programme in April 2017. 'For me, I really want to be part of the rebuilding process as it is a part of the game that I absolutely love. I fully expect it to be challenging because we are going to have to recreate a very strong, cohesive group, but saying that, I don't think you can underestimate the part that history plays in developing the players that want to recreate that. You cannot underestimate the strength that we have in our staff, and also the quality of the programme that we have. I deliberately took six months away from the game knowing that by doing that, and having had a long career, I would be able to come back in and give it absolutely everything because I still love playing.'

Although taking some well deserved time out, Danson admits that she had been keeping a close eye on what was happening during the trial and selection period for the new cycle, watching with interest to see which players would be coming into the programme.

'I was hearing amazing things about people not being able to sleep the night before the announcement because they were so desperate to learn whether or not they had made it. Players were celebrating with their families because it meant so much to them.' For Danson, it was a clear indication that the players joining the programme had the desire and hunger that they would need in order to succeed. 'You want players like that, people who are going to throw everything at being part of this programme. With players like that I think we have the capability to develop something pretty unique again.'

Live-wire attacker Lily Owsley, who was a European champion at 20 and an Olympic gold

medallist at 21, now finds herself being considered very much as a senior player within the group. 'We've had a huge amount of experience leave the programme, players who have been around for a long time like Kate (Richardson-Walsh), Macca (Hannah Macleod) and Crista (Cullen) who have been involved in numerous Olympic cycles,' said the University of Birmingham student, who has been joined in the central squad by team-mates Amy Costello, Olivia Paige, Erica Sanders

and Anna Toman. 'We do have players from Rio still around, such as Alex, and people like her are so integral for our future development as a group. Players like me, my experience is peanuts compared to some of the people who have left. I've only got four years of international experience behind me and some of those who have left had ten or more. We still have some very experienced players and we will need them in the leadership group, but it is a very different dynamic now to what we had before. We may have lost experience but we have got a lot of raw talent. The talent in this group is just immense.'

Owsley's position as a role model became obvious during an informal presentation ceremony to the new players ahead of their senior international debuts for England. Upon receiving their playing shirts, the newcomers were each asked to say a few words about what the occasion meant to them. 'A lot of them said that they had been inspired by what they saw at Rio, and it was really special to hear people who are now your team-mates say things like that, knowing that they want to repeat what we achieved out there. It is strange for me. When it comes to people like Eri (Erica Sanders), I would never think of myself as a leader over her, she's my team-mate from uni. Some of these girls are my best friends, and I desperately want them to be the best players they can be and for us to be the best team we can be.'

Star striker Alex Danson still loves playing and will 'give it everything' going into the Tokyo 2020 cycle.
Koen Suyk

Lily Owsley, a star performer for Great Britain and England in recent years, is now seen as a senior figure despite being just 21 when she won gold at Rio 2016.
Frank Uijlenbroek

For promising forward Erica Sanders, who joined the centralised programme after being a key player in the England Under-21 team and a prolific goalscorer for University of Birmingham, it is a period of intense excitement. 'To be training with people who have just won an Olympic gold medal is amazing and for us there is a lot to live up to. We clearly want to try to replicate what we saw in Rio, and knowing that they have done it does make it feel more achievable. I want to do exactly the same as they did, but clearly there is a lot of work to do. It is a huge step up for me. I only did one year of Under-21s and was lucky enough to go to the 2016 Junior World Cup in Santiago (Chile), but this is completely different. It is a big transition to senior level, getting used to the physicality, intensity and the pace of the game. We (England) played Germany in a test match and I quickly found out that it is so much quicker than any level I've played at before, and far more physical. I was mentally shattered afterwards, but I am slowly bridging that gap between junior and senior level.'

Another player who is central to the planned assault on the podium in Tokyo is the Rio penalty shoot-out hero Hollie Webb. She welcomed the new injection of talent and ideas; indeed she thinks change – and even disappointment – is crucial to future success. 'The new players coming onto the programme will bring something new, they already are. But that is how it has always been. The squad has changed its culture in the

Defender and penalty corner expert Giselle Ansley is another player from the Rio 2016 cycle who aims to be part of a potential Olympic title defence at Tokyo 2020.
Frank Uijlenbroek

England's Erica Sanders is part of the centralised programme for the next Olympic cycle.
Frank Uijlenbroek / Koen Suyk

Scotland's Sarah Robertson, in action here against Germany, is part of the Team GB centralised programme preparing for 2020.
Frank Uijlenbroek /Koen Suyk

years since I joined in 2013 and it has been constantly changing since 2004, and that is a good thing.

'We need new ideas if we want to win gold in Tokyo. The whole Rio cycle wasn't a successful cycle in a lot of ways, a lot of things went wrong. And I am not totally against us losing in order to win. I'm not saying that I want to lose matches but, if that meant losing in the final of the Commonwealth Games with just nine seconds to go in order to win in Tokyo, I would take that any day.

'The World Cup in 2014 was painful but it definitely helped us get stronger. And of course, we have to learn a new mentality now. We have become the hunted, not the hunters, and that is a very different place to be.'

While a successful defence of the Olympic title in Tokyo is clearly the end-game of the current cycle for Kerry and his new-look GB team, there is also the small matter of England's upcoming participation in a home World Cup to take into account. Hosted by England Hockey at London's Lee Valley Hockey & Tennis Centre in Queen Elizabeth Olympic Park, the Women's Hockey World Cup 2018 will bring together the best 16 teams in the world at what will be the biggest hockey event that the United Kingdom has ever seen. Although the 1986 Men's Hockey World Cup took place in London, it is the first time that the Women's World Cup has been played on British soil.

Simply hosting an event of this magnitude would have significantly raised the profile of hockey within the UK, but on the back of Team GB's gold medal success in Rio the interest has moved to an entirely new level. The home fans are expected to flock to the competition in their thousands in the hope of witnessing England storm to glory in the same stadium that they claimed the European title in 2015. While acknowledging the scale of the challenge, attacking star Sophie Bray certainly feels England have what it takes to create another moment of history by winning a first Hockey World Cup.

'We know what winning feels like and that gives you confidence,' said Bray. 'We have shown that not only at the Olympics but also throughout 2015 as well. We want to be the best in the world, and we'll do everything we can to achieve that at the World Cup. I'm as motivated as I've ever been. I look at the gold medals from the Europeans and Rio and know that I want to add more to the collection. I want to win gold not just at the World Cup, but also at the 2018 Commonwealth Games and then defend the Olympic title in Tokyo. To stand on the top of the podium is an amazing feeling and you want to do it all again.'

With the women's international teams of Scotland and Wales improving rapidly, there is also a sense of hope that England will not be the only team from the British Isles that will be competing at the major world level events like the Women's Hockey World Cup 2018 over the coming years. 'We (GB Hockey) need the other home countries to play in that environment,' said a hopeful Kerry. 'The more experience those players get playing the best teams in the world, the better they will be able to step into the GB team and play those top teams. With the World Cup, I really want the likes of (Scotland's) Amy Costello to experience that environment.'

While Kerry's comments about England's World Cup chances in London were echoed by GB and England Hockey chief Sally Munday, she was quick to point out that her focus was very much on the potential impact that the Women's Hockey World Cup 2018 could have on the future of the sport in the United Kingdom.

'I genuinely believe that we are at a tipping point for the sport here in the UK,' says Munday. 'I've said numerous times that one of our key goals is for us to become a nation where hockey matters. What do we mean by that? Well, we want people up and down the country, from those who know the sport and those who don't know it quite so well, to care about it and have an interest. The aftermath of Rio gave us a window of what it feels like to be a nation where hockey matters. For that three or four week period after the Games, everywhere I went I heard people talking about hockey. I sat on the train and heard people talking about the gold medal game. That is what we dream of. We want to be a nation where hockey matters because we believe that increased visibility will help us increase participation, which is great for the health of the sport and feeds more people into the talent pathway which will hopefully lead to more medals. With the World Cup, a revised international calendar and the build-up to an Olympic title defence in Tokyo, the next three years presents us with a chance to promote the sport like never before and we must make the most of it.'

GB Hockey women's centralised athletes for the Tokyo 2020 Olympic cycle

Nation	Name	Club (Jan 2017)	Position
+	Giselle Ansley	Surbiton	Defender
+	Grace Balsdon	Canterbury	Defender
+	Sophie Bray	Kampong (NED)	Forward
+	Charlotte Calnan	Surbiton	Midfielder
⊗	Nicki Cochrane	Beeston	Goalkeeper
⊗	Amy Costello	University of Birmingham	Defender
+	Alex Danson	Clifton Robinsons	Forward
+	Emily Defroand	Surbiton	Midfielder / Forward
+	Susie Gilbert	Reading	Midfielder
+	Takara Haines	East Grinstead	Midfielder
+	Sarah Haycroft	Surbiton	Midfielder
+	Sabbie Heesh	Surbiton	Goalkeeper
+	Maddie Hinch	SCHC (NED)	Goalkeeper
+	Jo Hunter	Surbiton	Forward
🏴󠁧󠁢󠁷󠁬󠁳󠁿	Sarah Jones	Holcombe	Midfielder
+	Kathryn Lane	Leicester	Defender
+	Joie Leigh	Clifton Robinsons	Midfielder
+	Hannah Martin	Surbiton	Midfielder / Forward
+	Shona McCallin	Holcombe	Midfielder
+	Lily Owsley	University of Birmingham	Forward
+	Livy Paige	University of Birmingham	Defender / Midfielder
+	Suzy Petty	Wimbledon	Midfielder
+	Ellie Rayer	Loughborough Students	Forward
⊗	Sarah Robertson	Edinburgh University	Forward
+	Erica Sanders	University of Birmingham	Forward
+	Zoe Shipperley	Buckingham	Defender
+	Amy Tennant	Großflottbeker (GER)	Goalkeeper
🏴󠁧󠁢󠁷󠁬󠁳󠁿	Roseanne Thomas	Wimbledon	Goalkeeper
+	Anna Toman	University of Birmingham	Midfielder
+	Susannah Townsend	La Gantoise (BEL)	Midfielder
+	Laura Unsworth	East Grinstead	Defender
+	Ellie Watton	Holcombe	Forward
+	Hollie Webb	Surbiton	Defender
+	Nicola White	Holcombe	Forward

Chapter 14

New Found Fame

Autumn 2016, one month after winning gold at Rio 2016, as she signed autographs for hundreds of fans at her local hockey club, St Albans, Hannah Macleod reflected on her new found fame. 'We're everywhere. We're just trying to get hockey out there for as long as possible.

'At the moment it's just volunteering time. Like here today, we've got 110 kids, we were supposed to only have 60, and lots of mums and dads have turned up too.

'This is the reception we've had all over the country. We've been getting out to Hockeyfest, which is an initiative that was set up prior to the Olympics after learning lessons from London 2012 about the best way to raise participation levels. It all helps capitalise on the success of our sport.

'The reaction and reception we have received really has been that spectacular. It's just breaking down the preconceptions of the sport. It's no longer jolly hockey-sticks, the game has evolved.'

For Maddie Hinch, her new found fame kept popping up in surreal fashion, 'A couple of weeks after we got back, I was in a pub, meeting the team from Red Bull, and I went to the toilet. Written on the back of the door was "Maddie Hinch is a hero"; then I was eating fish and chips another time and someone tweeted, "It's not everyday you see @MaddieHinch eating fish and chips". It really began to hit home then that life was going to be very different.'

If Macleod and Hinch were amazed that hockey was making headlines 30 days after the team won Olympic gold, they were flabbergasted when, six months later, the furore around the team's success was continuing. Far from simply being a case of turning up at clubs and running guest training sessions, the squad members were being invited to film premieres, awards ceremonies and television and radio shows. They were also picking up team and individual awards and had nominations in two categories at the showcase sports awards, the BBC Sports Personality of the Year Awards – as Team of the Year and, for captain Kate Richardson-Walsh, a nomination for Sports Personality of the Year.

'It went so crazy that we had to hire in a team of PR professionals to deal with all the media requests,' said England Hockey's head of communications, Craig Mortimer-Zhika, speaking in December 2016. 'Some of the players have had to engage their own agents because the interest has just gone through the roof.'

For different players, there have been very different stories and journeys. Compare Sam Quek's rise to television stardom – including a fourth-place finish on ITV's *I'm A Celebrity, Get Me Out Of Here* and a regular slot on Saturday night's *Play to the Whistle* – with

Georgie Twigg's quiet return to Bird and Bird, where she is a trainee solicitor. 'They (Bird and Bird) supported me for four years from 2012 to 2016, I felt I owed it to them to go back straightaway,' says Twigg, who returned to work just one week after winning Olympic gold.

'I would often be found getting changed after work to attend one award ceremony or another, but I haven't been out in the public eye as much as many of the others.'

The interest around the players saw the team members making an average of 78 public appearances each between September and December 2016. These ranged from school and club visits to guest slots on radio shows and appearances on television. There was also a trip to Buckingham Palace along with the other gold medal winners from Team GB. The enduring image from the visit was of Prince Harry joking with Susannah Townsend as she appeared at the palace on crutches following knee surgery.

Maddie Hinch, Hollie Webb and Kate Richardson-Walsh were guests alongside Hollywood 'A' lister Renee Zellweger on *The Jonathan Ross Show*; Sam Quek, Maddie Hinch and Alex Danson all sat alongside Phil Tufnell on BBC's *A Question of Sport*; for two people so used to being accomplished in all they did, Alex Danson and Maddie Hinch displayed an unexpected ineptitude in the kitchen when they appeared with Tim Lovejoy on *Sunday Brunch*; Helen and Kate Richardson-Walsh sang with Gareth Malone on the Christmas Special of *The Choir*; and Kate also appeared with Hollie Webb on ITV's star-studded *National Television Awards*, where the assembled throngs of actors and soap stars were treated to yet another airing of the final moments of the match and subsequent penalty shootout.

And despite the mantra that this was always about the whole squad, inevitably different characters have found themselves thrust into the limelight.

Possibly the two biggest stars, along with Quek, to emerge from the squad are the married couple Kate and Helen Richardson-Walsh. Since returning from Rio, the couple rarely left the limelight. There were newspaper interviews, appearances on television chat shows, Kate has become a regular contributor on Radio Five Live and also appeared on Radio Four's *Woman's Hour*.

For both the media and the public, the story of a married couple winning a gold medal provided an irresistible narrative and a story that went far beyond hockey. Newspaper article after newspaper article pointed out that this was the first married couple since 1920 to win gold at the same Olympic Games; others focused on the fact this was the first same-sex married couple to win gold. Wherever you turned, the Richardson-Walshes were front and back page news in the papers.

Athletes pose with their medals. ▶
Team GB Hockey

Lily Owsley, Shona McCallin and Sophie Bray at the athletes' parade in Manchester.
Team GB Hockey

Team selfie on the athletes' parade in Manchester.
Maddie Hinch / Twitter

In an interview with *The Guardian* newspaper (Sat 10 December 2016), Kate Richardson-Walsh said: 'Hockey has become a bit more front and centre. But, we must remember we are professional athletes. We're privileged in Britain to have lots of sports we're good at and we want lots of media coverage of that. I love sport, all of the sport, I want to read about it all. I think it's the time for hockey to try and wedge ourselves in there with the other big sports.

'You're not playing hockey to be a star, to be in the papers. But we want to do the very best job we can and we want people to see that. We go out into the country and talk about what we do, what it takes to be an Olympic athlete. We've shown our worth. As an association I think we're very well run. I think we should push ourselves.'

Despite the captain's words, the limelight was exactly where the squad repeatedly found itself. Over the three months following Rio 2016, the Team GB women's hockey team picked up five awards: BT Sport's Team of the Year; *The Sunday Times* Sports Women Awards Team of the Year; the Association of National Olympic Committees' Women's Team of the Year; the British Olympic Association's Great Britain Choice Awards; and the Sports Journalists' Association (SJA) Team of the Year. In addition, the gold medal shootout against the Netherlands was voted the BBC viewers' Moment of the Games.

For a team that was used to winning everything, losing out to Leicester City Football Club for the BBC Sports Team of the Year award was a blip in an otherwise perfect aftermath. 'It would have been nice to have won,' said assistant coach Karen Brown, 'but to be honest, just all being there was special enough. It was actually the first and sadly probably the last time that everyone who was part of the squad had been together since the final whistle went in Rio. Straight after the match we were all together waiting for the medals, but after that the athletes were all whisked off to various media commitments and we haven't all been together since. So SPOTY was as much about us coming back together as a group as anything else.'

There were also individual awards. Coach Danny Kerry was named BT Sports Coach of the Year and then he picked up the biggest honour of all when he was voted the International Hockey Federation (FIH) Male Coach of the Year. Karen Brown was honoured for the second consecutive year as FIH Female Coach of the Year and Maddie Hinch received FIH Goalkeeper of the Year. Kate Richardson-Walsh eventually finished sixth in the BBC Sports Personality of the Year, ahead of ten other high-profile sports stars, and as the second highest placed woman, behind Paralympic show jumper Sophie Christiansen but ahead of names such as footballers Gareth Bale and Jamie Vardy, gymnast Max Whitlock and Paralympic cyclist Dame Sarah Storey.

'It's a tremendous honour,' said an emotional Kate Richardson-Walsh, speaking to presenter Gabby Logan. 'We're so blessed in this country to have so many phenomenal athletes, and we're good at so many sports. To be here representing the squad of 31 amazing ladies and the hockey family, to be on this stage is a very proud moment.'

The media frenzy surrounding the team in those months leading up to December was unprecedented and award-winning former *Daily Mail* columnist Patrick Collins, president of the SJA commented: 'Confident, articulate and wondrously accomplished, the Great Britain hockey women made a dramatic impact upon the sporting year. A sport which has often struggled to secure the attention it deserves was transformed by the efforts of Kate Richardson-Walsh and her team. Their success demonstrated the enormous appeal of women's sport. And that appeal deserves to be reflected in the media coverage it receives.'

The icing on the cake for the squad was inclusion in the Queen's New Years Honours list and a trip to Buckingham Palace to receive their awards. For 15 of the gold medallists, it was to receive an MBE; for Kate Richardson-Walsh, who already had an MBE for services to hockey, it was an OBE that HRH Prince Charles placed around her neck.

Prince Harry and Susannah Townsend share a joke about the midfielder's injury.
Yui Mok / AFP / Getty Images

'When I was at school and thinking of what I might be one day, this was nowhere near my radar,' said Kate Richardson-Walsh, as she addressed a roomful of youngsters at yet another school visit.

'I wanted to be a physical education teacher and I would have been quite happy with that, but this is like being in a movie. It is quite bizarre. It is like what dreams are made of. I think it does show that, with hard work and if you really go for it, these things can happen to you.'

For Helen Richardson-Walsh, the MBE might never have happened as the letter had arrived while she was away. 'It's a funny story,' she says. 'I was away travelling. You normally find out with a letter through the post but because I was away, I hadn't replied. Myself and Kate were skiing in Whistler (Canada), I was on the ski-lift and my phone was ringing. I couldn't get the phone out in

time but I saw it was an unknown number. I then listened to a message from one of Buckingham Palace's people and that's how I found out! They just wanted to find out if we wanted to accept the honour. Obviously we did!'

From December through to April, the sight of hockey players arriving at Buckingham Palace was a weekly affair. Helen and Kate Richardson-Walsh received their MBE and OBE respectively from Prince Charles, with Helen commenting that it would make a nice addition to the mantelpiece. Maddie Hinch said that receiving the medal from Prince William was '100 per cent more nerve-wracking' than the shootout that led to Olympic gold. Shona McCallin said that she couldn't understand why team-mates kept texting her to see if she had any post – her MBE notification had been posted to her parents' address, while Lily Owsley kept the Queen waiting as she was in South Africa with the national team

Maddie Hinch collects her FIH Goalkeeper of the Year Award at a special ceremony in Chandigarh, India.
Frank Uijlenbroek

Maddie Hinch and mum Catherine grab a selfie at the palace after Maddie received her MBE.
Maddie Hitch / Twitter

on the day she was due at the Palace. In June 2017, it was announced that coach Danny Kerry was to be honoured with an MBE in the Queen's Birthday Honours list, alongside the man often credited with playing a key role in hockey's revival in the UK, Philip Kimberley.

While the publicity was great for the women and wonderful for keeping hockey in the spotlight, there was at least one person who was concerned at the effect all of the media attention was having. Back at Bisham Abbey, coach Danny Kerry was plotting the next four years, with his stated aim of 'winning as a winner' at the Tokyo 2020 Olympic Games.

'This (media interest) is something that I have not had to deal with before,' he said. 'I need to make sure that the returning players still have the motivation and hunger to be part of the squad. The challenge now is to combine emerging players with those that have been part of the programme for a long time. It takes a long time to get the culture and attitude of a squad right, so now it is a case of keeping stability through the players who are used to our way of working but injecting energy into the squad without unbalancing things.

'There will be people who inevitably drop off. When we won bronze in London, we didn't bring everyone with us onto the next phase. I am prepared to be brutal, I need to know the players still have the hunger and the motivation.

L-R: John-John Dohmen (Belgium - male player of the year), Naomi van As (Netherlands - female player of the year), Arthur van Doren (Belgium - male rising star), Maddie Hinch (Great Britain - female goalkeeper of the year), Maria Granatto (Argentina - female rising star), Laurine Delforge (Belgium - female umpiring award winner) and David Harte (Ireland - male goalkeeper of the year).
Frank Uijlenbroek

'It was right that they (the players) should enjoy their success,' he added. 'But they will really have to earn their places because I am dead set on winning again.'

When the new squad was announced in January 2017, there were some notable absences. Gone were the Richardson-Walshes, Crista Cullen, Sam Quek, Ashleigh Ball, Emily McGuire. Just these six athletes had amassed more than 80 years of international experience between them, with all the knowledge and insight that such experience brings.

'Yes, it will be tough to replace that sort of knowledge,' said Kerry. 'But my role is to look for the positives in that and to see change providing opportunity. When you chop down a tree, who knows what might grow in its place.'

One player who is dead set on continuing to amass the medals is double Olympian Laura Unsworth, who will be 32 by the time the next Olympic Games gets underway. 'The thought of going to Tokyo in 2020 and being part of a squad looking to defend the Olympic title is something that is exciting,' said Unsworth in conversation with her local newspaper the *Royal Sutton Coldfield Observer*. The paper changed its name to the *GOLDfield Observer* when Unsworth visited her home town in September 2016.

'We also have a home World Cup in London. At present, I am lucky enough to have Olympic and European gold medals and it would be a pretty cool achievement to try to add a World Cup and Commonwealth Games gold to make it a full set.'

And for fellow defender Giselle Ansley, the impact the squad has had on the country is an additional factor driving her quest for further glory. 'I have only cried once, and that was when these kids made an arch with their hockey sticks for me at Plymouth Marjon HC, my old club. But, we have gone out there and done lots because that was part of our vision. We want to get as many people involved as we possibly can. It has been amazing because we have seen the impact and, even more than the gold medal, it makes us realise what a very special thing we have done.

'The good thing about making history is that there is always something else to do. We want to win as winners, we haven't done that before; we want to win the 2018 World Cup, we haven't done that before. We also want to get that number one ranking. There is so much still to do. We just want to keep making history.'

Kate and Helen Richardson-Walsh at the Laureus World Sports Awards in Monaco.
Matthew Lewis / Stringer / Getty Images

Appendix 1: 'The 31 Centralised Athletes'

Throughout this book the athletes have made numerous references to 'the 31', the centralised group of Team GB women's hockey athletes that put in countless hours of training at the National Sports Centre at Bisham Abbey in preparation for the Rio 2016 Olympic Games. Their importance as a collective cannot be underestimated. The complete list of athletes can be found below, with their most recent club (at the time of writing) being listed first.

Name - Giselle Ansley
Nation - England
D.O.B - 31/03/1992
Clubs - Surbiton, Loughborough Students, Plymouth Marjon
Position - Defender

Name - Ashleigh Ball
Nation - England
D.O.B - 23/03/1986
Clubs - Slough, Bowdon Hightown, Bradford HC
Position - Midfielder

Name - Grace Balsdon
Nation - England
D.O.B - 13/04/1993
Clubs - Canterbury, Maryland (USA)
Position - Defender

Name - Sophie Bray
Nation - England
D.O.B - 12/05/1990
Clubs - Kampong (NED), East Grinstead, MOP (NED), University of Birmingham, Trojans, Surbiton
Position - Forward

Name - Crista Cullen
Nation - England
D.O.B - 20/08/1985
Clubs - Wimbledon, Leicester
Position - Defender

Name - Alex Danson
Nation - England
D.O.B - 21/05/1985
Clubs - Clifton Robinsons, Klein Zwitserland (NED), Slough, Trojans, Alton, Reading
Position - Forward

Name - Steph Elliott
Nation - England
D.O.B - 24/09/1990
Clubs - North Harbour (NZL), Holcombe, University of Durham, Roseberry
Position - Defender

Name - Amy Gibson
Nation - Scotland
D.O.B - 13/07/1989
Clubs - Reading, Surbiton, Slough, Old Loughtonians, Clydesdale Western
Position - Goalkeeper

Name - Susie Gilbert
Nation - England
D.O.B - 21/02/1989
Clubs - Midlands (NZL), Reading, University of Birmingham
Position - Midfielder

Name - Sarah Haycroft
Nation - England
D.O.B - 12/04/1991
Clubs - Surbiton, University of Birmingham
Position - Midfielder

Name - Sabbie Heesh
Nation - England
D.O.B - 06/12/1991
Clubs - Surbiton, Leicester, Loughborough Students, Bowdon Hightown, Cannock, Belper
Position - Goalkeeper

Name - Maddie Hinch
Nation - England
D.O.B - 08/10/1988
Clubs - SCHC, Holcombe, Leicester, Loughborough Students, Exmouth
Position - Goalkeeper

Name - Joie Leigh
Nation - England
D.O.B - 22/02/1993
Clubs - Canterbury (NZL), Clifton Robinsons, Cannock, Belper, Wakefield, Bradford
Position - Midfielder

Name - Kirsty Mackay
Nation - England
D.O.B - 16/11/1986
Clubs - East Grinstead, Bowdon
Hightown, Blackburn
Position - Goalkeeper

Name - Hannah Macleod
Nation - England
D.O.B - 09/06/1984
Clubs - St. Albans, Leicester,
Loughborough, Bedford, St Ives
Position - Forward

Name - Emily Maguire
Nation - Scotland
D.O.B - 17/12/1987
Clubs - Canterbury (NZL), Holcombe,
Reading, Kelburne
Position - Defender

Name - Shona McCallin
Nation - England
D.O.B - 18/05/1992
Clubs - Holcombe, Slough, Old
Loughtonians, MOP (NED), Beeston
(Nottingham Highfields)
Position - Midfielder

Name - Lily Owsley
Nation - England
D.O.B - 10/12/1994
Clubs - University of Birmingham, Bristol
Firebrands
Position - Forward

Name - Holly Payne
Nation - England
D.O.B - 11/07/1991
Clubs - University of Birmingham,
Leicester
Position - Midfielder

Name - Sam Quek
Nation - England
D.O.B - 18/10/1988
Clubs - Holcombe, Reading, Bowdon
Hightown
Position - Defender

Name - Helen Richardson-Walsh
Nation - England
D.O.B - 23/09/1981
Clubs - HC Bloemendaal (NED),
Reading, Den Bosch (NED), Leicester,
West Bridgford
Position - Midfielder

Name - Kate Richardson-Walsh
Nation - England
D.O.B - 09/05/1980
Clubs - HC Bloemendaal (NED),
Reading, SCHC (NED), Klein Zwitserland
(NED), Slough, Leicester
Position - Defender

Name - Sarah Robertson
Nation - Scotland
D.O.B - 27/09/1993
Clubs - Edinburgh University, Holcombe,
KHC Leuven (BEL)
Position - Midfielder/Forward

Name - Zoe Shipperley
Nation - England
D.O.B - 17/03/1990
Clubs - Team Bath Buccaneers,
Buckingham
Position - Defender

Name - Susannah Townsend
Nation - England
D.O.B - 28/07/1989
Clubs - La Gantoise (BEL), Canterbury
Position - Midfielder

Name - Georgie Twigg
Nation - England
D.O.B - 21/11/1990
Clubs - Surbiton, Clifton, Cannock,
Lincoln
Position - Midfielder

Name - Laura Unsworth
Nation - England
D.O.B - 08/03/1988
Clubs - East Grinstead, Holcombe,
Leicester, Loughborough Students,
Sutton Coldfield
Position - Defender

Name - Ellie Watton
Nation - England
D.O.B - 10/06/1989
Clubs - Holcombe, St Albans, Beeston, Cannock, Matlock
Position - Forward

Name - Lucy Wood
Nation - England
D.O.B - 22/02/1994
Clubs - Holcombe, Sevenoaks, East Grinstead
Position - Forward

Name - Nicola White
Nation - England
D.O.B - 20/01/1988
Clubs - Holcombe, Leicester, Slough, Loughborugh Students, (Brooklands) Poynton
Position - Forward

Name - Hollie Webb
Nation - England
D.O.B - 19/09/1990
Clubs - Surbiton, Beeston, Cannock, Belper
Position - Defender

Appendix

Appendix 2: Team GB Women's Hockey at the Olympic Games

2.1: Snapshot Summary

Number of Olympic Games attended: 7 (Seoul 1988, Barcelona 1992, Atlanta 1996, Sydney 2000, Beijing 2008, London 2012, Rio 2016)
Number of medals: 3 (Bronze – Barcelona 1992, Bronze – London 2012, Gold – Rio 2016)
Matches Played: 45
Matches Won: 23
Goals Scored: 83
Goals Conceded: 70

2.2: Olympic Placements

Rio 2016: 1st – Gold
London 2012: 3rd – Bronze
Beijing 2008: 6th
Athens 2004: Did not compete
Sydney 2000: 8th
Atlanta 1996: 4th
Barcelona 1992: 3rd – Bronze
Seoul 1988: 4th
Los Angeles 1984: Did not compete
Moscow 1980: Did not compete

2.3: Olympic Campaigns

Rio 2016
Final ranking: 1st - Gold
Pool phase (Round Robin): Team GB 2-1 Australia; Team GB 3-0 India; Team GB 3-2 Argentina; Team GB 2-0 Japan; Team GB 2-1 USA
Quarter-Final match result: Team GB 3-1 Spain
Semi-Final match result: Team GB 3-0 New Zealand
Gold medal match result: Team GB 3-3 Netherlands (2-0 after shootout)
Squad: 1: Maddie Hinch (GK), 4: Laura Unsworth, 5: Crista Cullen, 6: Hannah Macleod, 7: Georgie Twigg, 8: Helen Richardson-Walsh (née Richardson), 9: Susannah Townsend, 11: Kate Richardson-Walsh (née Walsh - captain), 13: Sam Quek, 15: Alex Danson, 18: Giselle Ansley, 19: Sophie Bray, 20: Hollie Webb, 24: Shona McCallin, 26: Lily Owsley, 28: Nicola White.

Non-playing reserves: Joie Leigh, Ellie Watton, Kirsty Mackay (GK)
Head Coach: Danny Kerry
Team GB Top Scorer: 5 – Alex Danson

London 2012
Final ranking: 3rd - Bronze
Pool phase (Round Robin): Team GB 4-0 Japan; Team GB 5-3 Korea; Team GB 3-0 Belgium; Team GB 1-2 China; Team GB 1-2 Netherlands
Semi-Final match result: Team GB 1-2 Argentina
Bronze medal match result: Team GB 3-1 New Zealand
Squad: 1: Beth Storry (GK), 3: Emily Maguire, 4: Laura Unsworth, 5: Crista Cullen, 6: Hannah Macleod, 7: Anne Panter, 8: Helen Richardson, 11: Kate Walsh (captain), 12: Chloe Rogers, 14: Laura Bartlett, 15: Alex Danson, 18: Georgie Twigg, 22: Ashleigh Ball, 23: Sally Walton, 28: Nicola White, 29: Sarah Thomas.

Non-playing reserves: Natalie Seymour, Abi Walker (GK).
Head Coach: Danny Kerry
Team GB Top Scorers: 5 - Alex Danson, 5 – Crista Cullen

Beijing 2008
Final ranking: 6th
Pool phase: Team GB 1-5 Germany; Team GB 2-2 Argentina; Team GB 2-1 New Zealand; Team GB 2-1 Japan; Team GB 0-0 USA
5-6 Classification match result: Team GB 0-2 Australia.
Squad: 2: Beth Storry (GK), 3: Lisa Wooding, 4: Anne Panter, 5: Crista Cullen, 6: Mel Clewlow, 7: Charlotte Craddock, 8: Helen Richardson, 9: Joanne Ellis, 10: Lucilla Wright, 11: Kate Walsh (captain), 12: Chloe Rogers, 13: Jennie Bimson, 14: Rachel Walker, 15: Alex Danson, 18: Sarah Thomas, 22: Jo Ellis.

Non-Playing Reserves: Katy Roberts (GK), Laura Bartlett*
Head Coach: Danny Kerry
Team GB Top Scorer: 3 – Crista Cullen

Replaced Jennie Bimson (injured) for the final three matches

Sydney 2000
Final ranking: 8th
Pool phase: Team GB 1-2 Australia; Team GB 0-1 Argentina; Team GB 2-2 Korea; Team GB 2-0 Spain.
7-10 classification crossover result: Team GB 3-2 South Africa
7-8 classification match result: Team GB 0-2 Germany
Squad: 1: Carolyn Reid (GK), 2: Hilary Rose (GK), 3: Kirsty Bowden, 4: Jane Smith, 6: Mel Clewlow, 7: Tina Cullen, 8: Kath Johnson, 9: Lucilla Wright, 10: Jane Sixsmith, 11: Rhona Simpson, 12: Denise Marston-Smith, 13: Helen Richardson, 14: Fiona Greenham, 15: Pauline Stott (née Robertson - captain), 16: Kate Walsh, 17: Mandy Nicholson (née Nicholls).

Head Coach: Jon Royce
Team GB Top Scorer: 3 – Mel Clewlow

Atlanta 1996
Final ranking: 4th
Pool phase (Round Robin): Team GB 0-5 Korea; Team GB 1-1 Netherlands; Team GB 1-0 USA; Team GB 2-2 Spain; Team GB 0-1 Australia; Team GB 3-2 Germany; Team GB 5-0 Argentina.
Bronze medal match result: Team GB 0-0 Netherlands (3-4 after penalty strokes)
Squad: 1. Joanne Thompson (GK), 2: Hilary Rose (GK), 3: Chris Cook, 4: Tina Cullen, 5: Karen Brown, 6: Jill Atkins, 7: Susan Fraser, 8: Rhona Simpson, 9: Mandy Nicholls, 10: Jane Sixsmith, 11: Pauline Robertson (captain), 12: Jo Mould, 13: Tammy Miller, 14: Anna Bennett, 15: Mandy Davies, 16: Kath Johnson.

Head Coach: Sue Slocombe
Team GB Top Scorer: 4 – Jane Sixsmith

Barcelona 1992
Final ranking: 3rd - Bronze
Pool phase results: Team GB 1-2 Netherlands; Team GB 3-1 Korea; Team GB 3-2 New Zealand.
Semi-Final result: Team GB 1-2 Germany.
Bronze medal match: Team GB 4-3 Korea (after extra time)
Squad: 1. Joanne Thompson (GK), 2. Helen Morgan (GK), 3. Lisa Bayliss, 4. Karen Brown, 5. Mary Nevill (captain), 6. Jill Atkins, 7. Vickey Dixon, 8. Wendy Fraser, 9. Sandy Lister, 10. Jane Sixsmith, 11. Alison Ramsay, 12. Jackie McWilliams, 13. Tammy Miller, 14. Mandy Nicholls, 15. Kath Johnson, 16. Susan Fraser.

Head Coach: Dennis Hay
Team GB Top Scorer: 5 - Jane Sixsmith

Seoul 1988
Final ranking: 4th
Pool phase results: Team GB 1-0 Argentina; Team GB 1-5 Netherlands, Team GB 2-2 USA
Semi-Final result: Team GB 0-1 Korea.
Bronze medal match result: Team GB 1-3 Netherlands.
Squad: 1: Jill Atkins, 2: Wendy Banks (GK), 3: Gill Brown, 4: Karen Brown, 5: Mary Nevill, 6: Julie Cook (GK), 7: Vickey Dixon, 8: Wendy Fraser, 9: Barbara Hambly (captain), 10: Caroline Jordan, 11: Violet McBride, 12: Moira MacLeod, 13: Caroline Brewster, 14: Jane Sixsmith, 15: Kate Parker, 16: Alison Ramsay.

Head Coach: Dennis Hay
Team GB Top Scorer: 2 - Vickey Dixon.

Appendix 3

3.1: Medal-winning Nations

Year	Venue	Gold	Silver	Bronze
2016	Rio de Janeiro (BRA)	Team GB (GBR)	Netherlands (NED)	Germany (GER)
2012	London (GBR)	Netherlands (NED)	Argentina (ARG)	Team GB (GBR)
2008	Beijing (CHN)	Netherlands (NED)	China (CHN)	Argentina (ARG)
2004	Athens (GRE)	Germany (GER)	Netherlands (NED)	Argentina (ARG)
2000	Sydney (AUS)	Australia (AUS)	Argentina (ARG)	Netherlands (NED)
1996	Atlanta, GA (USA)	Australia (AUS)	Korea (KOR)	Netherlands (NED)
1992	Barcelona (ESP)	Spain (ESP)	Germany (GER)	Team GB (GBR)
1988	Seoul (KOR)	Australia (AUS)	Korea (KOR)	Netherlands (NED)
1984	Los Angeles, CA (USA)	Netherlands (NED)	West Germany (FRG)	United States (USA)
1980	Moscow (URS)	Zimbabwe (ZIM)	Czechoslovakia (TCH)	Soviet Union (URS)

3.2: All-Time Olympic Women's Hockey Placements

Rio 2016: 1: Team GB, 2: Netherlands, 3: Germany, 4: New Zealand, 5: United States, 6: Australia, 7: Argentina, 8: Spain, 9: China, 10: Japan, 11: Korea, 12: India

London 2012: 1: Netherlands, 2: Argentina, 3: Team GB, 4: New Zealand, 5: Australia, 6: China, 7: Germany, 8: Korea, 9: Japan, 10: South Africa, 11: Belgium, 12: United States

Beijing 2008: 1: Netherlands, 2: China, 3: Argentina, 4: Germany, 5: Australia, 6: Team GB, 7: Spain, 8: United States, 9: Korea, 10: Japan, 11: South Africa, 12: New Zealand

Athens 2004: 1: Germany, 2: Netherlands, 3: Argentina, 4: China, 5: Australia, 6: New Zealand, 7: Korea, 8: Japan, 9: South Africa, 10: Spain

Sydney 2000: 1: Australia, 2: Argentina, 3: Netherlands, 4: Spain, 5: China, 6: New Zealand, 7: Germany, 8: Team GB, 9: Korea, 10: South Africa

Atlanta 1996: 1: Australia, 2: Korea, 3: Netherlands, 4: Team GB, 5: United States, 6: Germany, 7: Argentina, 8: Spain

Barcelona 1992: 1: Spain, 2: Germany, 3: Team GB, 4: Korea, 5: Australia, 6: Netherlands, 7: Canada, 8: New Zealand

Seoul 1988: 1: Australia, 2: Korea, 3: Netherlands, 4: Team GB, 5: West Germany, 6: Canada, 7: Argentina, 8: United States

Los Angeles 1984: 1: Netherlands, 2: West Germany, 3: United States, 4: Australia, 5: Canada, 6: New Zealand

Moscow 1980: 1: Zimbabwe, 2: Czechoslovakia, 3: Soviet Union, 4: India, 5: Austria, 6: Poland

3.3: All-Time Women's Olympic Medallists By Team

Country	Gold	Silver	Bronze	Total
Netherlands	3	2	3	8
Australia	3	0	0	3
Germany*	1	2	1	4
Team GB	1	0	2	3
Spain	1	0	0	1
Zimbabwe	1	0	0	1
Argentina	0	2	2	4
Korea	0	2	0	2
China	0	1	0	1
Czechoslovakia	0	1	0	1
Soviet Union	0	0	1	1
USA	0	0	1	1
Totals	10	10	10	30

*Includes West Germany

3.4: All-Time Women's Olympic Medal Matches

Rio 2016
Gold / Silver: Netherlands 3-3 Team GB (0-2 aso)
Bronze: Germany 2-1 New Zealand

London 2012
Gold / Silver: Netherlands 2-0 Argentina
Bronze: Team GB 3-1 New Zealand

Beijing 2008
Gold / Silver: China 0-2 Netherlands
Bronze: Argentina 3-1 Germany

Athens 2004
Gold / Silver: Netherlands 1-2 Germany
Bronze: Argentina 1-0 China

Sydney 2000
Gold / Silver: Argentina 1-3 Australia
Bronze: Netherlands 2-0 Spain

Atlanta 1996
Gold / Silver: Australia 3-1 Korea
Bronze: Netherlands 0-0 Team GB (4-3 aps)

Barcelona 1992
Gold / Silver: Spain 2-1 Germany (aet)
Bronze: Team GB 4-3 Korea (aet)

Seoul 1988
Gold / Silver: Australia 2-0 Korea
Bronze: Netherlands 3-1 Team GB

Los Angeles 1984
N/A (Round Robin format)

Moscow 1980
N/A (Round Robin format)

Legend: aps - after penalty strokes. aet - after extra time.
aso – after shootout

Team GB Women's Hockey Olympic Goalscorers

	Seoul 1988	Barcelona 1992	Atlanta 1996	Sydney 2000	Beijing 2008	London 2012	Rio 2016	Total
Alex Danson	-	-	-	-	1	5	5	11
Crista Cullen	-	-	-	-	3	5	1	9
Jane Sixsmith	-	5	4	-	-	-	-	9
Mel Clewlow	-	-	-	3	1	-	-	4
Lily Owsley	-	-	-	-	-	-	4	4
Kath Johnson	-	3	1	-	-	-	-	4
Helen Richardson-Walsh (née Richardson)	-	-	-	-	-	-	4	4
Nicola White	-	-	-	-	-	1	3	4
Susan Fraser	-	2	1	-	-	-	-	3
Mandy Nicholson (née Nicholls)	-	-	2	1	-	-	-	3
Sarah Thomas	-	-	-	-	1	2	-	3
Jill Atkins	-	-	2	-	-	-	-	2
Sophie Bray	-	-	-	-	-	-	2	2
Vickey Dixon	2	-	-	-	-	-	-	2
Mary Nevill	1	1	-	-	-	-	-	2
Rhona Simpson	-	-	1	1	-	-	-	2
Georgie Twigg	-	-	-	-	-	1	1	2
Giselle Ansley	-	-	-	-	-	-	1	1
Ashleigh Ball	-	-	-	-	-	1	-	1
Laura Bartlett	-	-	-	-	-	1	-	1
Christine Cook	-	-	1	-	-	-	-	1
Tina Cullen	-	-	-	1	-	-	-	1
Moira MacLeod	1	-	-	-	-	-	-	1
Denise Marston-Smith	-	-	-	1	-	-	-	1
Anne Panter	-	-	-	-	1	-	-	1
Kate Parker	1	-	-	-	-	-	-	1
Alison Ramsey	-	1	-	-	-	-	-	1
Chloe Rogers	-	-	-	-	-	1	-	1
Jane Smith	-	-	-	1	-	-	-	1
Sally Walton	-	-	-	-	-	1	-	1
TOTALS	**5**	**12**	**12**	**8**	**7**	**18**	**21**	**83**